S%@#!

And Other Four-Letter Words

That Every Child Should Know

J.K. Thomas

Youth Engineer

CONTACT

To schedule events for J.K. or for more information or other services go to:

WWW.WELLWHYNOTME.COM

ISBN: 13-97-8069287777-7

Acknowledgments

GOD ~ To my God: Thank you for the opportunity to use the gifts you have given me to share with those who may or even may not know you.

MOTHER ~ To my Mother: I could never repay or reward you for the man you helped me to become. Because of you through me, the world owes you a legion of gratitude. I love you more than there are droplets of water in all the oceans in the world. Thank you.

KIDS ~ To my Children: Rashad, Asia, Taylor and Kierin. Thank you for being who you are individually and collectively. I love you all. And to all the children and parents in my daycare and mentoring programs over the years, I hope I continue to be a good example for you.

DEDICATION

~ This book is dedicated to my wife.

~ Other than God, the true love of my life.

~ Thank you for your support,
understanding and love.

~ Thanks for your strength of a lion with
gentleness of a dove.

~ Continue to "Share My Life" with all of
love's jargon.

~ From the beaches of Mexico to the local
botanical garden.

~ You and God are all I live for to serve.

~ I pray that I am the man that you
definitely deserve.

INTRODUCTION

"There is always some kid who may be seeing me for the first time. I owe him my best."

Joe DiMaggio

"It was a dark and stormy night." I had already had a very long week. In addition to taking care of my bedridden father suffering from vasculitis by myself, I was running two businesses. Earlier that day I had had two business meetings. See, I am also a firefighter, and I knew I was going to be at the firehouse for at least a couple of days straight and had to make sure that everyone, including my mother of course, was O.K. The date was August 26, 2011. Heavy rain and gusty winds had already signaled the prelude to Hurricane Irene coming to shore. The storm had already ravished the Carolina coast. The death toll was 6 in North Carolina and 4 in Virginia...and now it was Maryland's turn.

From the time that I arrived at the firehouse house around 6:00 p.m. until 2:00 a.m., we responded to what we call, "chump calls": Babysitting downed wires. Pumping water out of people's flooded basements. Rescuing people "trapped" in their cars with four inches of water on the road. Guarding transformers that had caught on fire. Transporting people, of all days, to the hospital for hang nails and stubbed toes...All-in-all, a total of 32 calls in an eight-hour period. Still very exhausting. Once again, this was on top of all I had done earlier in the week and earlier that day. But finally, I was able to go to bed. I don't think I could have taken another call anyway. I was spent. Though the bunk bed at the station isn't the best, it was the best that night. And it felt good. I was mentally and physically tired. All 37 trillion cells in my body said, "We're done for the day, Brother Thomas." Not to mention the emotional fatigue...My father had already had his first stroke in April of that year, and little did I know that in three weeks he was going to have a second stroke that was going to cause paralysis on his whole left side. My mind was done...There was no way I could do any more that day...The National Weather Service said that the brunt of the storm was yet to come. It was to hit at 3:30 a.m. It didn't matter. The ONLY way I was getting out of that bed was on the second coming of Christ. . . So I thought.

3:33 a.m. The firehouse alarm goes off and jolts me out of my sleep. "Alert standard rescue box; 14-7; 8600 block of Keller Avenue. House collapsed. Report of people trapped. Respond on talk group 22." Within three

2

minutes, I, with our rescue squad, was out the door. The rain was no longer coming "down"; it was coming sideways. Downed branches all over the road, for whatever part of the road we could se. The roads were inundated, and visibility was only about 75 feet in any direction. It had not been like this when I went to bed only an hour and a half ago! I was looking at the street lights, and torrents of water splashed up into lights. Never knew that street lights could look submerged in the air...Suddenly, the squad came to an abrupt stop...There was a huge tree in the middle of the road, blocking all lanes. We immediately jumped out of the squad, grabbed our Stihl chainsaws and started cutting away at the massive tree in the roadway. Cutting and dragging...Cutting and dragging. That's all I remember doing....Of course, now visibility was about 4 feet since we were out of the squad. Water rolling off the brim of my helmet like an overflowing bathtub...But within 5 minutes or less (hard to be sure exactly) we were back in the squad, on our way to the rescue scene. As we were driving down the road, each tree bent with its own personality to tease us. Each tree with a goal it seemed to grab our rescue squad; then at the last moment it changed its mind and bent in another direction. The wind's howling, more like sinister laughter, mocked us as the trees taunted us. Finally, we arrived. Upon arrival, I saw a woman standing on the side of the porch of a white house....Seeing no one else, this must be our "trapped" victim....Everything must be O.K. I approached her. She looked like Sissy Spacek in the last scene of *Carrie* at the dance. "Are you O.K.?" I asked her.

"I ran to the neighbors and pounded on the door, but I didn't get a response," she said. "So I ran back and was able to get into the kitchen, where I had my cell phone, and called 911." She gasped out of breath, shaking and trembling through tears....and still not answering my question.

"But are you O.K.?"

Still trembling. "It's not me. It's my fiancé."

"Well, where is he?"

Her wet, unsteady hand pointed to the house. "He's in there."

I turned around and really saw nothing. There were several trees on the ground and up against the house. "He's in where?" I asked, trying to figure out where she was referring.

"Our bedroom is under all those trees."

Readers...trust me. There was no visible room. There was barely a house. It was like that moment in a movie where the scene is still but the lens stretches and elongates the still shoot. Pointing to the mountain of trees, I yelled back to the guys, "Hey, she's saying her fiancé is in there somewhere." We approached the rear of the house. We could barely see what was supposed to be the bedroom, which was an added room behind the house. I guess he could hear us because he started yelling. But all we could see were trees and debris which lay on top of him. All we could do was hear him.

We, with other units of the County soon arriving, went to work. After using several 2-D strut ART's, saws, ratchets, chains and cribbing to stabilize the house and surrounding large fallen trees, we were able to reach the trapped victim. We mentally fought through the uncertain results, including the cacophony of storm sounds around. Deafening wind. Pelting rain sounding like acorns falling from a 200-year-old oak onto glass. Haunting cracking and snapping of trees and branches as if a T-Rex were walking through the distant woods. Hundreds of yards of electric and cable wires were swinging between arching and waving poles, animated as if they were competing for a double-dutch world record. Then...90 minutes later . . .the patient was extricated. By 6:00 a.m. I was finally in bed from my work week, my long Saturday and now, technically, Sunday morning.

The MIND. Before I get into the heart of this book, I wanted to talk about the number one "four-letter word". Yes. All the other four-letter words in this book are very important, but they are all predicated on the health and condition of the mind. In my rescue experience, I was convinced that I was physically, mentally and emotionally tired. I had nothing else to give. But when that firehouse alarm sounded and it was time to push all three of those elements again, I acted without any effort. Now, one may argue that it was adrenalin. But there is also the argument of the conditioning of the mind. In society we see it all the time.

How many millions of times daily does this happen? Parent driving home. About to make the turn down her street. She is revisiting her day of how much her boss got on her nerves. How she spent all day in heels and hourly touching up her make up trying to impress a troupe of men, not one of whom is even her husband. She's driving in a blank stare, but her mind is racing on how bills are going to get paid. Is she going to be late with the car note this month or the rent? Though fruit is a healthier choice, for the same $6.00 she can buy a case of Ramen noodles....She pulls up to the house. Walks inside. Her son runs up to her. "Mom!...I need the money for picture day tomorrow. And I need to be at soccer practice by 5:00." (The time now is 5:10 and practice is on the other side of town.) Oh! And I still need the materials for my project..." (which is due tomorrow). Then this same parent suddenly finds energy that she declared she didn't have. Money she didn't have. Time she didn't have. And runs little Mookie to wherever he wants to go. Is this adrenaline? Is this maternal instinct? Or is this conditioning of the mind? Maybe even mind control. How does one go from certain mental and physical fatigue to going another 5 hours...Then getting up the next day and doing it all over again. Granted, people do over exert themselves and suffer from exhaustion; however, I believe it's a lot deeper. Most of us have heard the Chinese proverb:

"Be careful of your thoughts, for your thoughts become your words. Be careful of your words, for your words become your actions. Be careful of your actions, for your actions become your habits. Be careful of your habits, for your habits become your character. Be careful of your character, for your character becomes your destiny."

Destiny comes from the middle 14th century word *destinare,* meaning "that which has been firmly established." Therefore, if we have already been firmly established, our mind, thoughts, and actions are really just road blocks to what's already in us and not steps to reach our destiny.

Is your glass half full or half empty? It doesn't matter if your glass contains opaque, malodorous, polluted content. The journey from your mind to your destiny can be compared to a coronary artery. Your blood at birth flows naturally. (In other words, you haven't been blinded by the world yet.) But when your arteries start to become diseased (disease is the narrowing or blockage of the coronary arteries, usually caused by atherosclerosis) these plaques can restrict blood flow to the muscle by physically clogging the artery or by causing abnormal artery tone and function. Without an adequate blood supply, the heart becomes starved of oxygen and the vital nutrients it needs to work properly. This can cause chest pain called angina. If blood supply to a portion of the heart muscle is cut off entirely, or if the energy demands of the heart become much greater than its blood supply, a heart attack (injury to the heart muscle) may occur. In other words, "what has already been firmly established" inside of us starts becoming clogged with things from the outside, things we chose to put inside of us.

Peace of mind is a natural condition, and is available to everyone. One way "peace" is defined is "a state of harmony." Harmony is a state of agreement and accord. So when we have peace of mind, our mind is in agreement in all aspects to live the life we want to live. But in order to have this peace of mind we have to take care of it. Though it's never too late, we have to take care of our minds so that we can take care of the minds of our children as early as possible, from birth if possible. A healthy mind strengthens and supports our children's ability to have healthy relationships, make good life choices, maintain physical health and well-being, and discover and grow toward their potential. A healthy mind will help them to receive the other four-letter words that they should know in this book and the volumes to follow.

THE NUMBER FOUR. The number four itself has universal meaning as well as overall principles that I'm trying to share with children and those who are working with children. The Number 4 symbolizes the principle of putting ideas into form, and it signifies work and productivity. The Number 4 represents a strong foundation and stability. One of my goals is to transform the mindset when one hears certain "four-letter words". The meaning of each "four-letter word" in this book, *any* four-letter word for that matter, is based on the meaning one gives it. But too many of our thoughts of what we consider and accept as facts and truths about certain words are really other people's definitions and truths and not our own. The number four symbolizes the ability to use practical thinking, basic form of order, prepare for renewal, instinctual knowledge. Four is also the number of fate, so it must be remembered that there will be many things that happen over which you have no control. But with the proper mindset it's not what happens to you but how you respond after it happens to you.

Biblically, the number four also derives its meaning from creation. On the fourth day of what is called 'creation week' God completed the material universe. On this day he brought into existence our sun, the moon, and all the stars (Genesis 1:14 - 19). Their purpose was not only to give light, but also to divide the day from the night on earth, thus becoming a basic demarcation of commemorate time. They were also made to be a type of signal that would mark off the days, years and seasons. And how many seasons are there? This question brings me to another point that we have to get children to understand as we share the four-letter words that they must know...Seasons in life are going to change. There's a time to plant. There's a time to cultivate and work. There's a time to harvest. And in the winter, things die off. There's that time to reflect, deciding to get rid of what's not working and starting over. But it's also a time to celebrate the hard work from the spring, summer and fall. . . if you worked. The good news is that if a child didn't harvest well, because he had nothing to work on because the seed wasn't planted, guess what always comes after winter? That's right, spring all over again. The problem with most children (especially teens) is that they stay stuck in winter. They plant once...work once...try to harvest it and don't get the results that they want; then instead of winter being just a season, it becomes a way of life.

The earth is divided into four cardinal points: North, South, East, West. There are the four witnesses of God on earth, miracles, wonders, signs and the gifts of the Holy Spirit (Hebrews 2:4). Our children can experience the miracles of this life, the wonders all over this beautiful world, the signs of love and compassion from others and the gifts of grace and forgiveness from the Holy Spirit.

If you're an adult and are reading this book to share with children, be careful because you, too, will have to do what I'm asking children to do after reading or being exposed to this book. How can you expect a child to listen to you if you're not willing to do the same thing? A child has to be able to respect the source of information. **(1) What is your willingness to learn?** How open are you truly to accept what you may read and to do what you need to do to have the life that you claim you want to have. Children very early on sincerely claim what they want but quickly are more interested in having fun during class than being a human sponge to take in everything that the teacher has to say. Once again, the mind has to be trained or transformed to be non-distracted and nonnegotiable with the willingness to learn. Which leads to number 2. **(2) What are you willing to give up to learn?** You can't say that you want one thing so badly and not be willing to give up a certain T.V. show, or high-end designer clothing, or socializing with your friends nine hours a day. This means adults and children. Maybe it will mean getting that cell phone plan that's $19.00 a year instead of $19.00 a week, or having children play video games once a week instead of once a day. **(3) What is your willingness to accept**

change? In the words of Jim Rohn, "If you want things to change, you have to change." Things will never...ever... EVER... become better just by standing still. The key word here is accept. People, especially children, always will look at this as something they are losing instead of a temporary or even permanent change to get what they ultimately want. There are "4" main (but not *only*) categories where people of all ages struggle; and because they struggle, they fail. Number 1 is the ability to change where they spend their money. Number 2 is the ability to change where they spend their time. Number 3 is the ability to change what foods they need to stop and start eating. Number 4 is the ability to change the people they hang around. Technically, you could stop reading the book right here! But you've already purchased the book and I offer no refunds after you've cracked the spine of the book...Lol. If you read the book all the way through, then you already have some level of willingness to learn. Also, you were willing to give up some time that would have been spent somewhere else. But the last one is going to be the hardest; that is, you truly want what you want. Change your mind to get what you want, or change what you want. The two cannot exist together.

I have one final note to my young audience before I end my introductory remarks: Remember to respect your parents and teachers. You can ask questions if you don't fully understand why something is the way that it is without insulting and questioning the source, especially if the source has what you are aspiring to attain. Think about it. How dare a child disrespect a teacher and the teacher has her own paycheck...the child doesn't. A teacher has her own car...A child doesn't. A teacher has her own place to live...A child doesn't. A teacher has the choice to leave and work anywhere she wants in the world...A child doesn't. Being a teacher may not be a child's goal, but until a child can at least do the minimum of what I listed a teacher can do, he should button his lips, sit down, and listen to everything that his teacher has to say and offer; and then go home and study and master it.

And to all:

"I've learned that people will forget what you said, people will forget what you did, but people will never forget how you made them feel."

Maya Angelou

Maya Angelou, whose birthday is 04/04, voiced these words of wisdom, and I have carefully thought about every word that is in my book and how those words will make you feel. If I can make you feel different about yourself, create more self-value and more self-worth, then this book would have been worth my effort. Think about your most precious memories. Do you really remember what was said or just how the event or person made you feel? I want you to feel triumphant, proclaiming a Latin phrase that my Grandmother feebly whispered on her deathbed. This Latin phrase, coincidentally, has three "four-letter words." This is what I want you to declare about every obstacle, every life challenge, every constructive goal, every ambition, every aspiration and with every passion: ***"Veni, vidi, vici"*** . . . I came...I saw...I conquered!

PAIN

Should people like pain? Why do some people like to suffer? Don't we all want to feel good? Why do some people want to feel bad? Before you think that these are ridiculous questions, think about how someone you may know, maybe even yourself, may be living right now. We say that we don't like pain but we daily make choices to stay in situations that we find unpleasant. I live in the State of Maryland. Perfect State if you ask me. It has a balance of all seasons. It really bugs me when people complain about the cold. One, it's not cold all that long as it is in New England or Alaska. Two, if you don't like it, then move. It's Maryland. It's going to be cold a few months out of the year. If you've lived in any state for a year or more...and you don't like that particular city or state, then move. Complain about the state after you've moved, maybe, but not while you still live there and you're doing nothing about it. This is the human condition for most in most aspects of our lives. We say in the presence of our children that we don't like certain things, such as politics, retirement, or the neighborhood; but our children are also seeing that we are doing nothing about those things. So why should they do anything about things they don't like? They will also adopt the complacency complaint syndrome that you have and just continue the family cycle.

The very first question was, should we like pain? The answer is yes...In the early stages of life or a major project, I'm sure most of you have heard Jim Rohn's quote: *"We all must suffer one of two things: The pain of discipline or the pain of regret."* Of all of Mr. Rohn's quotes, this one has to be among the top three most-true statements. Still, it falls short in registering in the minds of both children and adults. The reason why this quote fails to register with children and adults is not necessarily because we are conditioned to think that we're undisciplined, but because we have forgotten the "no pain, no gain" mantra from the 1980's. The "no pain, no gain" catchphrase was impactful when it pertained to physical exercise, and it is equally powerful today when it comes to building character or setting benchmarks for success. Our society stresses too much on pain avoidance. The results of the pain of discipline are always less harsh than the results of the pain of regret. ALWAYS.

Here are the points we must work with children to make them understand the importance of and the difference between the pain of discipline and the pain of regret. There are two keys for all these points. One key is the time you spend with the child to go through the process and discipline with them. The second key is to focus on the end goal or desire. Start with small disciplines with the child and make a big deal of the accomplishments. It is crucial to celebrate. And here's the life-long action as the adult, we have to celebrate with the child even if the end result isn't exactly how they pictured it to be.

With the pain of discipline comes:

1) **The sacrifice in the things that you enjoy.** Not that they can't enjoy the journey, but kids must understand that in order to be as good as they want to be in school, sports, or any other commitment, it most likely will require them to turn off the phones, computers, T.V.s and video games. It may require their missing some play time.

2) **Requires unwanted and unscheduled action.** A child needs to understand that he may have to get up early or stay up late to get certain tasks done.

3) **Mandatory assessment.** A child must be taught to be truthful of where he is presently in life. It goes with a phrase I say a lot in my seminars: "The hardest thing in the world to do is to tell the truth about yourself."

4) **Consistent planning.** Map it out. The younger the child, the fewer the steps. At least 3 but nothing more than 7. If the discipline desired is over a year for a teenager, then it can be more. This is so you can perhaps use a monthly plan.

5) **Learning.** Any discipline and end goal is going to require research and reading of the subject. Have your child journal and date notes and the process.

6) **Persistence.** It builds value in what a child is after. But the main thing it builds is patience. Children have

a major problem with patience. This is natural. Keep in mind, from out of the womb it was all about them. Therefore, it is hard to teach them the discipline needed for persistence.

7) **The word NO!** In our society, we have a tendency to think that everyone has to be happy. We are afraid to upset or disappoint anyone. As adults, especially parents, we want to be able to say yes to children as much as possible since we were denied or said no to a lot when we were kids. But in a constructive manner, saying NO more than saying yes could be the most powerful word for success to a child. So we YES to a lot more than we should. Staying true to your goal may mean saying NO or YES to people. Teach children that if someone is a true friend, he will understand and be there for you after the project or task.

For middle and high school students, teach them how to own the room. Good stage presence. Teach them confidence. There are so many people that think that just because they buy a new suit or dress, the confidence will magically appear. We already have enough over-priced suited reticent and withdrawn clods of men and women. Especially men! Enough! Confidence has very little to do with what you look like. If you obsess over that, you'll end up being disappointed in yourself all the time. Instead, confidence comes from how you feel in any moment. Posture. Eye contact. Speaking only when necessary and with sense. You don't have to speak perfect English but teach kids to avoid slangs, colloquialisms and the "ummms". Walk into a room acting like you're in charge, and spend your energy on making the people around you happy. Giving confidence to others will come back to you and you'll end up feeling better about yourself.

I can't stress enough the importance of making a child feel comfortable. The fact that he at least tried, he doesn't have the pain of regret even if he fails. When you dare to embrace an opportunity but fail in your attempt, you can still walk away with your head held high.

Now it is important to be honest with children as well. Don't scare them but be honest if a child does not go through the pain of discipline. Whether an adult will admit it or not, there will be the pain of regret. FYI: The showing of pain of regret as an adult often does not come out as a direct admission. It is usually masked by the following beginning phrases: "I wish I had…". "If only I had more money, I would…". I would have gone but…". "I would if I had the money". "I would go, but… If you recognize any of these, stop using them…at least around kids anyway if not for yourself.

"Whoever loves discipline loves knowledge, but whoever hates correction is stupid."

Proverbs 12:1

In being honest with children, you must let them know about the possible regrets as well if they do not discipline themselves early in life. Here's the list of regrets one will face at or approaching the end of their lives:

In the end, you'll regret...

1) ...the chances you didn't take.

2) ...the relationships you should have built or fixed.

3) ...the time you wasted on making the decisions that you should have made a lot quicker.

4) ...not saving more money and not having started sooner.

5) ...not taking more time to do nothing.

6) ...wishing you cared less about people's opinions at an earlier age.

Children are far too smart at such a young age to start being the "thing" to get in their own way. The world is going to throw enough at them. They don't need to bring additional negative blocks in their developmental stages. It is mandatory to grab them early to prevent them from experiencing the pain of regret. If a child doesn't understand the difference between the pain of discipline and the pain of regret, then he will miss opportunities to succeed in life. Our souls, and not so deep down, always know what to do. The challenge is to silence distractions and rid the mind of already-embedded ideas and influences of perhaps well-meaning friends and family.

Here's another way of looking at "the pain of regret". The pain of regret can, and is, almost always longer than the pain of discipline. What kids must understand is that Pain itself is not harmful. It is a necessary process of life when it's presented as discipline. The pain of discipline, once taught, exampled, and accepted, though uncomfortable at times, becomes the foundation to essential development. However, the pain of regret often becomes chronic and sustained and can affect the body both physically and emotionally. Think about a person with pain in general. If you bang your knee on, let's say, a table, yes it is an inconvenience and you may hobble around for a while. You may even have to stop and sit down for a bit. But eventually you'll be back on your feet and on your way. The pain of discipline. But let's say you hit the same knee in a way that cracked your knee cap but you kept walking on it. But instead of resting or taking care of it, you kept walking on it. After a while, the pain will wear you down, draining your energy and sapping the motivation for whatever walking task you may have been trying to accomplish. The pain of regret.

According to the Integrative Pain Center of Arizona, many people with chronic pain develop depression-like symptoms: lack of interpersonal interaction, difficulty concentrating on simple tasks, and the lack of desire to simplify their life as much as possible, which often manifests as seeking isolation and quiet. Sleeping often makes the pain less intrusive, and that, combined with the exhaustion that pain induces, means that it isn't uncommon for a person to start sleeping upwards of ten hours a day. Is this you? Does any of this sound familiar? Do you want the children you raise or work with go down the same path? Some recent studies have also shown that chronic pain can actually affect a person's brain chemistry and even change the wiring of the nervous system. Cells in the spinal cord and brain of a person with chronic pain, especially in the section of the brain that processes emotion, deteriorate more quickly than normal, exacerbating many of the depression-like symptoms. Though it starts off as internal, triggered by emotional and social response to the pain of regret, over time it becomes physical. It becomes more difficult for people with chronic pain to process multiple things at once and react to ongoing changes in their environment, limiting their ability to focus even more. Sleep also becomes difficult, because the section of the brain that regulates sense-data also regulates the sleep cycle. This regulator becomes smaller from reacting to the pain, making falling asleep more difficult for people with chronic pain. This is how the pain of regret is disguised in our society today. So what are we to do? What are we to teach the children on how to adopt the pain of discipline?

Teach a child to ask himself these three questions when getting ready to make an excuse to fall off task.

1) Would I believe this excuse if anyone else besides me was saying it?

2) Does this excuse even make sense?

3) Am I really going to let this excuse stop me from what I want to do?

But to have a child build up to this new way of thinking about pain starts with the adults. Are you committing the equivalent of fourth hand smoke in your daily encounters? You're asking, fourth hand smoke. What is that? We've all heard of second hand smoke. This is the smoke that is inhaled by a person standing near another person smoking a tobacco product. Third hand smoke is breathing the residual smoke that lingers on clothes, furniture and one's breath. fourth hand smoke is the life-long effect after the first three are gone. Are you negatively committing fourth hand smoke to the people you meet daily? Daily you directly or indirectly run into more people you don't know than you do know. What kind of image are you leaving? Adults don't have to be perfect. But children and the people around us will notice even the slight tenacious positive change in our lives. So let's get to it. Pick one thing and make a slight difference. One-tenth could be the difference between Silver and Gold. One inch could be the difference between champion or losing team. One drop can be the difference between pure gold and an alloy. One step by you could be the difference of a child living a successful life or a mediocre life.

You and your child need to stop making unworthy people a priority in your lives. Stop entombing your lives in the opinions and the insignificant acceptance of others. Don't let your happiness depend on something that you may lose. This could be relationships or material things. Don't entertain these relationships or material things at all. Don't get involved and think you can just resist them. Just avoid them all together.

For now on in your transition, **P.A.I.N.** should stand for: **P**ause. **A**void. **I**nward. **N**eglect. So right now. Stop. Pause. Evaluate where you are right now in your life. Evaluate yourself and your child's life. No longer neglect what your true desires are. No longer neglect who you and your child were born to be or what you are capable of conquering. Trounce the ordinary mainstream of the lives and cattle-driven herd around you. Embrace that you were given a life...and are strong enough to live it to its fullest.

*"Everything you do is based
on the choices you make.
It's not your parents,
your past relationships.
your job, the economy,
the weather, an argument
or your age that is to blame.
You and only you are responsible
for every decision and
choice that you make. Period.*

Wayne Dyer

SAVE

Just in case you were wondering, yes, this is actually, technically, the title of the book. Though all the four-letter words are very important, this one has more of an impact than our society realizes. The power of saving impacts not only our lives but our children's children's lives. Another phrase for save is "creating generational wealth." Think about it. Many of the names we know today, Ford, Rockefeller, J. Paul Getty, Joe Kennedy, Sr., Johnson and Johnson, every Arab oil company, Mars Candy, Walmart [Walton], Forbes and DuPont, just to name a few, have saved money well to spend their money well to create their fortunes. For some, this is after they lost tons of money in early ventures just to save money again. Not to take anything away from their ingenuity, hard work, tenacity and vision but thousands of people have made millions of dollars over the years. But it's the ability to **save** and reinvest that created the wealth they were able to pass down to their children's children.

Now granted, most of the companies that made their wealth were built at or soon after an opportune time, i.e., The Great Depression or even more so, slavery. Slavery is often referred to as the engine that built the American economy. But the key was to save. Think about where you would be if your family 20 to 30 years ago saved even $25.00 a week...How about even $10.00? Making children understand the importance of money is a very important, on-going and daily responsibility of parents. Once children understand the importance of money they can make wise decisions relating to money matters in their perspective life. Therefore, it is very critical to make children understand the importance of money at the right time. Such maturity amongst them relating to money matters will definitely help them achieve more in life.

Today's parents aim at providing for their child, meeting each and every need. It is the, "I want my child to have better than I did when I was a child" syndrome. As such, the child may not be aware of the financial difficulties which are faced by parents. Therefore, it is very essential for parents to make children understand the importance of money. They don't have to be all in your money business every day; however, if they learn to respect money at the right age, they will definitely grow-up as wise and financially responsible human beings. Here is how you can teach children the importance of money.

1. Use different envelope / jars / boxes.

Many are familiar with the envelope budgeting system for their own money, but this can also work for children. On either envelopes, jars, or boxes, have your child draw a picture, paint or decorate what he or she wants. This will make it fun. You may even want your child to attach pictures from magazines or the internet of what he or she wants to save for. Since a child is more tactile and visual this will help him to stay on task. For example, the short-term savings container might have a picture of a specific toy, while the long-term container might have a picture of a trip to Disneyland. Teach your child to set aside money for short-term and long-term goals, and have another container or envelope for spending on everyday items. Also, a lot of arts and crafts stores make blank puzzles. Assist your child to download a picture, let's say, of his favorite Star Wars action figure whom he wants to meet at Star Wars Land at Disney. Attach the picture to a 100 piece blank puzzle. With an X-Acto knife, trace all the puzzle pieces with the glued picture on top. When completed you should have 100 Star Wars Disney puzzle pieces. Now let's just say the total cost of the trip is $5,000 and there are 100 pieces to the puzzle. That would mean that each puzzle piece represents $50.00 As you save each $50.00 closer to the trip, your child or the family can attach a new puzzle piece.

2. Make a saving goal chart.

Once you know what your child wants to save for, figure out how many weeks it will take, and print out a chart. Notice I said weeks. Anything more than 90 days for a young child and he will get either bored or frustrated. On the printed chart you can let each box represent a week and your child can put a sticker in that box once the money for that week is earned and set aside. If you have an older child, a simple marker would do or you can be creative and even hot glue pennies in the boxes as the money is saved. Maybe simulate a pictograph. Each penny represents $1.00 or $5.00. If you don't want to waste real money, you can always use fake money. Put the fake money on the board, but the real money is in the bank.

3. Offer rewards for saving money.

Consider rewarding your child (younger child) for saving his or her money. By the time a child is 10 she should be taught to be able to see the value of savings without the pat on the back or reward. But for a younger child, if your child doesn't spend any money for a certain amount of time, provide a small reward or treat. You can also make the prizes better the longer your child saves. Try stickers or reward coupons, an extra 1/2 hour of video games, toys, or whatever motivates your child.

4. Be an example in not only saving but showing that you are saving.

One of the best things you can do is let your child see that you save money too. You may have heard the old adage, "People prefer to see a sermon rather than hear a sermon." Once again, since a child is so visual, to see you put money in a jar then drive it to a bank is critical. Put money in a jar while your child is watching and tell him or her it's your savings jar. This will show your child that saving is "normal." Plus, since most young children want to be like their parents, seeing you do it will provide them with money lessons that further inspire them to save. If there's a suit or a dress that you want, show the money going from the jar then to the store. This will give a child a chance to see examples of patience and to see money actually building to something that can be purchased later. Here's the coolest thing to do...Don't worry about the thank you letters after I tell you this. I'll already know the impact this will do. But thanks anyway. Have your child see you put money away every day or at least once a week in the jar. When you get to let's say $100. Let your child sit with you to pay a very small bill. Something no more than $40.00. Then take your child to church to see you put $10.00 in the plate. Then let him see you put $10.00 towards an investment fund...maybe to buy Disney stock or something. $20.00 to take him to the movies. (Matinee I'm sure for $20.00) Have him witness you buy your spouse flowers or at least do something for another family member. Then have him give the last $10.00 to a homeless person or drive down to a shelter or your local Ronald McDonald House and physically drop off the money. NO ONLINE DONATIONS. There's a lot more power in physically dropping off of the money. Then as they say in the hip-hop world, "Drop the mic!" Your child just experienced everything from your having patience to save the $100 to how to spend it. Do that for a year and see what that does for not only your child, but you as well.

As your child gets older, a goal chart may be less inspiring, and drawing pictures on an envelope tends to lose some of its charm. Therefore, as your child grows, here are a few more ideas to teach him or her about saving:

Now let's get back to the money break down. As early as 15 a child must change his / her mindset of dividing money. If you've done what I suggested in the previous paragraphs, it shouldn't be hard for him / her to grasp. The key here...a child must have the concept and embrace retirement at this age as well. Depending on the compounded interest rate, hopefully something that will on average yield 7%, if a 15 year old puts away only $20 a week consistently and does not touch it at all, he will have over a million dollars by the age of 45. Try to find a middle class 45 year old that has a million dollars liquid cash separate from any other investments he may have invested in through his company. And still have 20 plus years before the official retirement age. A 15 year old may say, "45! That's such a long way off." At that point you'll let him know how fast the 30 years will pass.

Here's an updated chart for teens to follow for every dollar he / she receives.

Whatever 35%	Just Because 5%	Reinvest in Self 10%	Give 10%
Emergency 5%	Larger special items 20%	Retirement 15%	

Whatever ~ This is literally for whatever they want! Have them still think about responsible spending like maybe clothes, cell phone, class ring etc. But this is also money for gas, for going out, movies, eating out, gifts for the holidays. This will help them to understand that if they have $35.00 remaining of the $100 out of a paycheck, they shouldn't blow $34.00 dollars of it on song downloads alone and then have no money for a school field trip.

Just Because ~ This is the random act of kindness percentage; it is the power of random giving, especially something that involves money. This is different from giving to the "I'll work for food" panhandler or the giving to your church or local charity. This giving is to people you know; maybe it could be recognizing and appreciating them for something they've done for you or even something you recognized that was done for someone else.

Self ~ This percentage, though it's only 10%, may be one of the most important. This is the money that is spent on personal development and growth. As Jim Rohn said, "If you want things to get better, you have to get better." Because the world is always changing, you must change just a little bit faster. The world is always spinning; therefore, you have to spin just a little bit faster. The world doesn't reward average; the world rewards the bold, the courageous and those who are willing to challenge themselves to be master contributors to society. You must reinvest in yourself. The world, or even worse, "The Man" is not going to help you build you. You need to take control of it yourself. The more prepared you are, the more you must give.

Give ~ Now this is the giving for church offerings. If for some reason you don't go to church, then give to a good reputable nonprofit organization.

Emergency ~ This is more important than people realize. This is for that time when you suddenly need a new radiator, your roof fixed, when they have to dig up your whole front yard for drainage emergencies. The reason why this is so important is because when these events occur... and they always will... most people dig into their normal paycheck budget or some other savings allocated for something else and just throw off everything. To keep from coming up short on your car payment, house payment or any other essential bills or savings, start an emergency account right away consistently; and when an event happens, you'll already have the money set aside for it.

Special ~ This is the saving for a house...Not an apartment fund. Or maybe even buying a car outright. Not financing. Vacations are not under this category. Vacations would fit under the "self" category.

Retirement ~ If you're one to believe in such a thing. This is where you would put aside money for this. Just remember to diversify your portfolio. When your child is old enough to understand the concept of interest, you can look for savings accounts that earn interest. Help your child open a high yield account online and explain the importance of compound interest. I don't really believe in retirement, so you can also call this **Freedom money,** meaning that through proper investments and managing of money, the interest alone that you earn from the principle is enough to pay for your lifestyle.

As we draw this four-letter word to a close, here are a few other points to help your child save.

5. Help your child prioritize.

The older a child gets, the more he wants...Have an older child write out a wish list of things he or she wants to spend money on and prioritize that list. Ask your child to think long-term as well. How about a nice laptop for college, a graduation trip to Costa Rica, or even the down payment for a house someday? And we can't forget the big one. A car. But not just any old car for $200 off the street and for an extra $50 the seller will throw in the steering wheel. Select a car that will need little to no repairs; but if a car is financed, emphasize the importance of making a big down payment. Then, have your child allocate an amount of his allowance or "income" to each goal. These are the beginnings of a financial plan and this type of thinking will serve your child well in the long run.

6. Let your child make mistakes.

Most of the time, the best lesson comes from a poor decision, especially when your child is young and the financial loss won't be so great. Sometimes the lesson comes from a no decision. This is where the, "If only I had..." statements come in as adults. But we want to avoid the no decision mistakes as much as possible. Small goals missed are O.K. but there are thousands of teens each year who have big goals to go to college or to start a business but didn't think enough to or were encouraged enough by a parent when they were younger to save even the smallest amount of money. Most parents will have to force a child to put away money. I've never seen or heard a child 5, 10, 15 years down the line regret a parent for forcing them to save his money the years prior. Usually the best and quickest way to show a child or teen the "mistake" lesson is right after the holidays. Most children always wish they could have bought more or a bigger gift for a family member or friend. There may be opportunities to review the previous year and remind a child of his spending expenses. "Remember that toy in May you just had to have?..." "Remember in August all those times you insisted on going to Burger King?..." "Remember I told you to get the cheaper jeans from Marshalls but you just had to have the latest design put out by 'Lucky' Jeans?..." Reminding a child of some purchasing "mistakes" made earlier may help him to make better choices in the coming year.

But the main point to understand about making mistakes is that its O.K. when it happens and you can't let it get you down. The problem most adults have when they make a mistake is that they get emotionally distraught and then they never make a financial decision to get restarted or continue in their financial quest or goal.

7. Play games.

There are a number of games available to teach financial, business and money concepts to children. Monopoly and The Game of Life, for example, can teach money management skills as well as the importance of planning ahead. Rich Dad 'Cashflow' for Kids is another good option focused on money management. In addition to classic games related to money that you can use as family game night ideas, there are a number of online games as well such as Rich Kid Smart Kid.

8. Teach your child that he/she should use a credit card only if he can pay the balance off in full each month.

A couple of summers ago I was returning home to Maryland after spending a week in Arizona for a Jack Canfield Seminar. By the way, if someone tries to tell you that the heat isn't bad in Arizona because its "dry heat", they are lying. because 113° is and totally feels like 113°. About two thirds through the flight, I noticed that the plane started to descend. Flying back and forth between the east and west coast as many times as I have, I knew this was way too early for a landing at BWI. Within 5 minutes, the Captain came onto the radio and announced that there were electrical and computer problems at BWI and we had to take a detour and land in St. Louis, Missouri. Of course when we landed, passengers not only from our flight but several other flights scrambled to get a new flight to their final destination. Now this happened on a Saturday morning.

My next flight out...Monday! Most of my liquid cash was spent from my Arizona trip. Though on my bucket list of 100 things to do, visiting St. Louis was easily 168. Luckily, I had a credit card that I could use and comfortably stay at a nice Comfort Inn near the airport, dine moderately, catch a Cardinals baseball game, site see, and go into The Arch. It ended up being quite a rewarding diversion. But what made it really nice was that I had more than enough credit to handle it. Then when I got home, I just quickly paid it off. A credit card is a great thing to have mainly for true tight financial immediate binds. But once again, if you have saved your money as suggested, you should have the liquid money at home in your account to quickly pay right back off the credit card balance. Teach kids that the following things do not count as emergencies to use a credit card: Clothes. Eating out. Clothes. Phone. Clothes. Gas. Clothes. Trips. Clothes. Movies. Clothes. Nails. Clothes. Hair. Clothes. Gifts. Clothes. Skating. Clothes. Candy. Clothes. Shoes. Clothes.....Did I leave out anything....Oh how could I forget? Clothing. Duh?

One credit card is enough. Help your child shop around for the best card. A lot of teens get excited at the first card that comes their way. Tell them to relax and just have a conversation with them about the card. If he plans on traveling a lot, maybe a card that can build a lot of traveling reward points. If there is a lot of driving for a job or school, maybe a card with gas reward points. Don't forget about looking at the interest rates. It may only be 0% for the first 90 days but then inflates to 24% for any purchases and even higher for cash advancements. Building credit is a good thing in the early years of one's life but it must be done responsibly and even planned out.

9. Talk about money and legacy.

While you may not want to discuss your salary in front of your children, you may want to let them hear you discuss your financial plan and the arrangements you're making for retirement, for example. Also, the real conversation you want to have with your child is about leaving a legacy to them. One of my best friends lives in South Carolina. He is looking into buying property to grow a tree farm to leave behind to his four kids. Depending on the type of tree he may be able to do one good cut in the remaining of his life time. Sell the wood and pay off the property. The rest of the time is training his sons to take care of the property for after he is gone. He may not live long enough to profit from the investment himself, but by training his children mentally, physically and financially, his successors will be taken care of for years to come.

So to SAVE is very important. And the great thing about saving is that you do not have to be rich or even just well-off to be very successful and to get great results. When saving, a child has to answer what is very important to him, and society. The biggest lesson and concept for him is going back to the "PAIN" chapter. The "pain of discipline" of saving money or the "pain of regret" of not saving money or saving properly. Unfortunately, money is one the major components of the formula of the definition of life that everyone must face. The reason why I said unfortunately is because you would think and hope life would be based on giving, loving and serving each other. But the formula we exist by is **L=C(EmEc)^2** (**L**ife is equal to our **C**hoices times our **E**motions times **E**conomics squared.) Our choices are based on either logic (neocortex), feelings (limbic) or our gut (reptilian); times the emotional story we attach to that choice, times the economics of the world. And both are magnified a lot more than we give attention to in order to live a fruitful life. After a while, even giving, true love and serving will come down to your emotions and economics. Just one big example, in a marriage, the CHOICE of infidelity or even divorce is usually based on the emotions and the economics of one or both parties, and not on giving, serving or loving the way that they used to, that is, if those bonds had existed in the relationship in the first place.

We can go on and on about the power of saving. The take home rule: It is never about how much money you make. It is always about how much money you keep. The better your saving, the better choices you will make, the more confidence you'll have, the better your relationships. The better you'll feel emotionally, the better you'll feel physically, the more impact you will have in your church and community. SAVE is so important, that it made it to the cover of this book. So that should tell you something. So start today. Not your next paycheck or income tax refund or when you hit "the big one" of the next Powerball that breaks $300 million. You'll find out quickly that in order to say YES to save, you'll have to say NO to something else. And if you're saying, "This is good stuff and I'll start with my child right away!" well, as I always say, kids will listen more to what you DO than what you SAY. So guess what parent, teacher, mentor, or adult! Get to SAVING! We as adults can't keep saying that, "We're living our lives for the children." When we don't show them that we are even living our lives for ourselves.

TIME

Three things you can't recover: words...moments and TIME...What is time? It depends on whom you ask: God...a person on death row...a teenager...a person with a terminal illness....a newborn baby...a first kiss...an Olympic swimmer or track runner.

Our lives are daily dedicated to "getting our time back". We are told to go to school to get a job good enough to retire as early as possible so that we can spend the last 5 to 20 years of our life with our "time", which by that time will be full of aching joints or organs not working the same as they did when you were 15; a time when we will be boasting a bank account not suited for a Third World peasant and exerting the energy of a cat that has just used up its 8th life. And the same thing continues from generation to generation.

What makes time so precious is that we don't know how much of it we really have. I always cringe when I hear of a young person dying. Here I am in my forties and I feel that my life is just beginning. To think of a teen or a twenty- something dying floors me. The thought of someone born after me and dying before me I always have a hard time grasping.

For the purpose of this book, we'll look at time as an asset, a bartering tool, and a one-time use resource.

MATERIAL ACQUISITION: People like stuff! And often, if possible, we want the best stuff. Usually the top three are houses, cars, and technology. I just watched a story on TV where a famous singer spent her summer off the coast of Italy on her yacht. [Her fiancé had his yacht there too, only about 100 yards away] They were saying that it cost $340,000 a week to rent and maintain the yacht. That is not including the $40,000 dollars a week in fuel. People spend so much time on trying to obtain stuff. Though the "stuff" is also sometimes a better education, items for elderly parents, donations to a church or a non-profit. Having stuff is great. I'm trying to get my stuff as well. But at what cost. When someone is lying on his death bed, he is not wishing for more stuff; he is usually wishing for the time back that he actually had but squandered so that he can spend time with their children, his spouse, the gym, the church, better friends, tropical destinations, hometown locations, the perimeter of the grocery store for better food choices. If one focuses on gaining stuff, then he is in jeopardy of losing the stuff that really matters.

EDUCATION:

"Great minds discuss ideas; average minds discuss events; small minds discuss people."

Eleanor Roosevelt

I could write a whole book on this quote alone. But for kids and teens, I narrowed the use of time down to just two categories: education and the use of technology and social media.

As I mentioned in my first book, the word education comes from the Latin word *Educare.* This word is the combination of the root form *"e"* or *"ex"* which means "out" as in the words "ex"it and "ex"odus; and the root form *ducare* which means "to lead" as in air "duc"ts. So, parents who wish to educate their children will "lead them out" of the shadows of doubt about a career and into a clear path that rewards their talents and interests. True education traverses both smooth and rough terrain. The terrain may get rough when the child changes his mind several times on career choices. Still, his time should be spent moving forward or educating himself in a career choice. How can anyone say he wants to be something and not do anything towards it? As parents or adults, we realize that the age of the child, will, of course, determine what and how much we should ask of them; but in any profession, there is always something to do and to learn. I teach a lot of times that traditional formal education is meant to support what it is that you really want to do. Formal education is not supposed to dictate where to go or tell us what to do.

For some parents, education is nothing more than a glorified name for a babysitter while they go to work. For other parents, it is something to obtain: Go get   an education." Sadly, education has no personal definition for these parents, not to mention their children.

But let's look at *education* from its true meaning, which is to "up-bring" or "to nourish." One of the most priceless feelings in the world is to be nourished or cared for. Children love the caress of their parents. People pay hundreds of dollars a year for massages. Women look forward to the pampering in a pedicure chair. Even ancient kings and queens loved to be fed exotic fruit while being fanned by their servants. Nourishing is how education *can* be. However, sometimes education is an up-bringing that blazes rough terrain and requires daily care in order to navigate over uncharted or bumpy paths. To up-bring means to let fail on occasions. It means embarking on adventures that are way beyond the boundaries of one's daily surroundings. This often results in the rewiring of the emotions because emotions are what really drive us. The rough adventures are those unexplored territories of science, culture, human behavior, philanthropy, geography, anthropology, and the arts. Rough up-bringing means to let one feel the anxiety in competition and the world spinning at one's feet when lying still. Successful up-bringing is not just telling, but showing that the water, the sand and sunsets at Virginia Beach are different from the water, sand, and sunsets at Jalicia Beach in Puerto Vallarta. True education goes beyond brick and mortar. It is knowing when one should be in a crowd, and when it is okay to be alone. It is knowing when it's okay to be loud and when it's okay to be quiet and patient. It means showing respect and exercising social civility, even when the rules are not written down. Your child will always feel your presence and your hand guiding him to the right decision, and he will know that he has your heart for support whether you are physically there or not. Conventional education can never come close to this. Most successful people who have achieved what they desire on a higher level have true education as described above. But here's the bring-home thought: If you noticed, most of the above education description did not require a whole lot of money, if any money at all. It is all about the time. It is all about the time. It is all about time that must be used wisely in the pursuit of true education.

"You can't produce a baby in one month by getting nine women pregnant."

Warren Buffett

HEALTH: At the end of the day, all that we really have is our health. It doesn't matter how much money is in your bank account. It doesn't matter how many material things you possess. It doesn't matter what great dreams and aspirations that you may have. If you do not have your health, everything you desire or presently have will be limited or even nonexistent. What use is it to have all these goals, and dreams and you're not around to see them or fulfill them. Now if that wasn't enough to convince you, how about this for those of you who have children? You say that you love your children. If this is true, why don't you take care of your health? Children often come across as inconsiderate, spoiled, self-centered and materialistic, but if you were to die or become violently ill, they would trade in every cell phone, PlayStation and XBOX for your health or return to life, or even to have just one more day with you. Well, that one more day can start now. Your food choices or even lack of exercise could be the time that you are throwing away spending time with your children...your spouse...your pet...best friends. One of my favorite places to sit and just listen to God's creation all around me are the beaches in Guanacaste, Costa Rica. To cut myself short of even just one of those trips because I chose to eat fast food 8 days a week, or refused to walk around the block for my health is unthinkable.

We make time for everything but our health. But without it, everything else doesn't matter or soon won't. There are 168 hours a week. You mean to tell me that what you personally desire your children, your spouse, your church, your friends, your legacy is not worth 5 of those hours a week? That includes coming and going: 15 minutes to get there, 30 minutes in the gym, 15 minutes to get home, 5 days a week. You're working two or more jobs so your children will have a better life, but your health is deteriorating. I understand that we all want a better quality of life for our parents, children and loved ones and money is often a great assistance in that, but we really need to reconsider our priorities and spend the time to take care of our health.

LIFE AFTER DEATH: Residual effects of our time are probably the most crucial. I know none of us asked to be here. But since you are, what can you do to make it a better place? The first question really should be, "Why should I?" Besides the 400 trillion to one odds you faced to even get here in the womb, think about all that has had to happen or not happen in the history of the world for you to even exist, even down to every street light that was caught or not caught. The choices that everyone else made or did not make in the history of the world, big or small. Every piece of trash thrown on the ground. Words and music have vibration so every positive or negative sound you say or play. Every hug. Every kiss...hand shake...Hitting or kicking is a transferring of energy so every hit or kick out of anger. Every action completed from of a negative thought or idea. How about every time you lie to the universe and say you're fine when really "fine" for you stands for "**F**reaked Out, **I**nsecure, **N**eurotic and **E**motional."? (from the movie, *Italian Job, 2003)*

Every choice that you make from the time you wake up until the time you sleep should be to continue positive energy after life. The world was given to you in a beautiful way before you were born, who are you to transform positive energy to negative energy with what you make, say or do. Whether you were born in the mountains of Malibu or the mountains of Peru, or whether you were kept in platinum crib or a decrepit manger, this world was a beautiful place. Stop giving energy to people and things that don't matter, which is pretty much almost everyone and everything. The existence of this world was not based and does not care about your petty negative feelings, or an event, or a person. Your measly trillion of negative cells to the centillion of other cells in this world and universe. The universe doesn't need it. So stop creating it.

Now there is what's called the butterfly effect. If enough positive or negative energy and choices are made, they can start to affect the world through a trickling down affect. We are starting to see this in our air quality and global warming. Recently I saw a story on TV about the effects of fracking in Oklahoma causing earthquakes. Oklahoma was doing just fine until the fracking industry introduced the pumping of water deep into the crust of the earth. Now Oklahoma has gone from barely having earth quakes to having hundreds of mini earthquakes per year.

"If you don't make the time in creating the life you want, you're eventually going to be forced to spend a lot of time dealing with a life you don't want."

Kevin Ngo

So, pertaining to time, what do you teach kids to do? What's the mindset that would apply to everything? I heard a saying once that, "Oysters don't need sun screen." In other words, don't waste time with the things in life that don't really matter. Well, how do we do that? TIME. I mean this in two ways. We must be mindful not only of the time we spend with our children, but also of the time we spend away from our children. What we do on our own time *away from* our children makes an incredible impact on the quality of communication we offer when we are *with* our children. One frequently noticed example is the profanity that we use when we are not in the presence of children. Parents, a lot of times, are telling their two-year-old not to use foul language, but they use it themselves! Then one day, it slips out:

"Boy! Haven't I F@#% told you not to use that Mother F@#% language?" I'll beat your F@#% A$$ if I hear that S%@# again! Now go to the frig. and get me a D@mn beer."

Now you may be laughing because you've heard this...Or it may be you. Then you're wondering why little Mookie 15 years from now is cursing you out for not letting him stay out past midnight on a school night. This is just one example. I go over a lot more in my seminars and workshops, but you get the idea. You may have to stop, as they say, "cold turkey" and do it the way it's supposed to be done for what's best for you and your family. Cultivate wholesome language practices and healthy social activities when you are not with your children.. They aren't going to pay your bills. They aren't going to leave a genealogical or financial legacy for your children. They aren't going to pay for your house, vacations, food, clothing, education, transportation or anything else. Look out for you and beyond.

When I started writing this chapter, I had just recently gotten married. For several months before the wedding, my wife-to-be spent a lot of time planning, designing, redesigning, buying, returning, tasting, re-tasting, missing plenty of sleep. Both of us spent plenty of money for 200 people who swore to be in attendance at our wedding. These people said they wouldn't miss it for the world. About twenty didn't show, with no notice; and ten others called or contacted us the day before or the day of the wedding simply saying they would not be able to make it. One of my guests and close friend had a brain aneurism. Now that's a good reason. No one else had a reason, not to mention a good one. But did they care about how much time and money for the caterer and everything else was spent based on their word and "confirmation" of their coming? NOPE! That's fine. The point is most people are ALWAYS, in the end, going to do what's best for them regardless of what you may think or what you may have done and regardless of what you think you are owed and deserve. So starting today, you need to do the same.

**"If you don't have time to do it right,
when will you have time to do it over?"**

John Wooden

Now the definition of "right" will obviously change from household to household. But if you don't make any effort at all, I can tell you right now that you're doing it wrong. Average people find a way to spend time, great people find a way to use time. Time is what we want the most but waste the most. Though time is free, it can be most costly if not used properly.

You will be defined on how you spend your time. What if you and your family could spend four weeks a year in an over-the-ocean glass bottom bungalow on a private island off the coast of Fiji. People will notice and will judge you on that. No matter how you're dressed or how you speak, but if you live in Baltimore and your idea of going out of town on a big vacation is the fifty- minute ride to Washington D.C., people will judge you on that. If your phone rings during church hours, what does that say to people about how you normally spend your Sunday mornings? If your phone doesn't ring, it's because people already know that between the hours of 8:00 a.m. and noon (3:00 if Southern Baptist, Lol) not to even bother calling because you've already put out there that that's church time for you. People will judge you on that. And we could go on and on. But you get the point.

Some of the most wasted time is the energy spent on the past. No one is saying you have to like what happened in the past or accept the end result that the outside influence wanted you to conclude about what happened in the past. But to talk about it constantly and to spend emotional time and energy is not only a waste of time, but also a detriment to your physical health. Every second dwelling on the negative past is also a second squandered, a second not focusing on and building your future. Please get in your head and teach this to your child: Once time is gone, it's gone. **FOREVER.** Do not waste a single moment.

Until you change what you do daily, you'll never experience that one moment in the sun. The adage, "If you want things to change you have to change. If you want things to get better, you have to get better." (J. Rohn) Think about every professional athlete and movie star, musicians, Oprah Winfrey. I'm not talking about the one-hit wonders but the Stevie Wonders, Not the Fly-by-Nights, but the Gladys Knights. Think about what they had to change daily in order to achieve success and happiness. Now you may say I'm not in life for all that flash and fame. That's fine. But you still cannot keep doing what you're doing to reach a better life. **The same life that you wake up and wish for every day, if you had invested time wisely, you may have already had it**. Read the book by Marshall Goldsmit**h,** *What Got You Here, Won't Get You There*. **For you and your child, in the beginning this may mean many lonely days and nights. Your head may become bloody, but keep it unbowed.**

Just like climbing a mountain, the oxygen may be thin, it may be cold, it may be slippery, you may question your journey, you may lose some fingers and toes along the way, but your heart, your soul will make it to the top. And *that*, my friend, is what ultimately matters.

"Short as life is, we make it shorter with careless waste of time."

Victor Hugo

Until you value yourself you won't value your time. If something or someone doesn't make you spiritually stronger, healthier, happy, a better person or financially more secure, then don't give it or him your time. This is very important and not to be taken lightly or carelessly because you can share this information with a child, and the next thing you know he and ten of his buddies are playing PlayStation online. And you'll ask, "What is going on?" His response would be, "You told me to do things that make me happy and to better someone else's life." So go deeper with what's truly important in life. What may be paradise to one person in Aruba is simply just home to someone else in Aruba. Get to the core of what happiness truly is. Work with a child to find happiness in standing still. In patience. In giving. In working. In humanitarian efforts. In doing more than what's expected. In doing more than being paid. Here is where you'll find your true value to yourself, family and the universe and not a value given to you by any man, woman, culture or organization.

"Now is the time ..."

(2 Corinthians 6:2)

Have you ever thought about investing in time? Making time work for you? What do you mean, Kelvin? Well, glad you asked. Though the details and the process may take a while, only because of your present mindset, the concept is very simple. Yes. Time is time. Everyone on this earth has the same 86,400 seconds a day. But then why is it that some are happier and or more successful than others? About 1- 5% do have that financial advantage, so I will give them that. Another 15% have a cultural advantage. The rest...we have to create and leverage ourselves so that while we are doing one thing, money, time and opportunities are also being created somewhere else. For example, if 'The Man" owns a multi-million dollar business, let it be known that if he or she is at the golf course, he is not just catching some sun and exercise, he is creating other deals. On that day their company may be making $30,000 a day, but on this day next year it's up to $90,000 a day because while they are paying employees pennies to make the $30,000, the owner is making deals and networking with others to increase his or her revenue. We can do the same on a smaller scale. First, every time money comes your way, save some and invest some. And yes, they are two different things. Second, build on strong relationships. What will happen is that while your child is mastering traditional education, people with whom you've built strong relationships are also looking out for your child. The phone will ring from friends and family on workshops, internships, once-in-a lifetime getaways, jobs, about seminars, needed grants, excursions, letters of recommendation, exclusive tours, pilgrimages, links, peregrinations, hook ups and expeditions. These are all people indirectly spending "time" working for you while you're fulfilling other engagements. So, here's a hint: Build relationships with people who can help you with your future. Build relationships with people who have what you want. Build relationships with people who are physically and obviously where you want to be. Why would you waste your time talking to someone who claims he can make you rich and can have you driving an Aston Martin, but he is driving around in a Civic?

Now, is the time to go, regardless of your present circumstances, income, education, relationships and self-imposed feelings, and make the change you need to make. You live only once. Each second that is presently passing comes only once and never to return.

**"We say we waste time, but that is impossible.
We waste ourselves."**

Alice Bloch

LOVE

Love
So many people use your name in vain…
Love
Those who have faith in you sometimes go astray…
Love
Through all the ups and downs the joys and hurts…
Love
For better or worse I still will choose you first

Chorus Lyrics by: Musiq Soulchild

Everyone has heard of the seven types of love: Agape, Eros, Philautia, Pragma, Ludus, Storge, and Philia. If not, Google it. But this powerful four-letter word pertains to children not only being successful but also maximizing their potential. You may see some overlap of the six types of love with the love I'm displaying in this text, but by the end it will stand alone as one of the top four-letter words that all children should know. And as Musiq Soulchild said, "Hopefully, we will get children to choose love first."

In 1st Corinthians 13:13, the apostle states that of the three gifts, faith, hope and love. The greatest of these is love. Love exists in everything in this world. Whatever the object is, you may not love it, but someone does. You may not like grapefruit, but someone does. You may not like Budapest, but someone does. You may not like spiders, but someone does. You may not like *Star Wars*, but someone does. (Actually, most people do.) You may not like taphophilia, but oddly enough someone does. So getting a child to understand the concept that everything that was created was with love in mind, whether we agree with it or not, will also give the child the foundation of respect for other people's goals, desires, and points of view. This will also help immensely in engaging in productive conversations. Ultimately, by keeping conversation open, a child will have a better chance to achieve what he or she has set out to do.

Though love should always be chosen first, love is still just the second most powerful emotion. You'll find out the most powerful one in volume 2 of this series. Everyone in the world has experienced love at some point. It may have been at birth. It may have been in the form of an elementary school crush. An actor on T.V. A musician. A first true teen or adult romance. This love could have been in the form of giving or receiving. The giving of love is just as powerful as the receiving. A child has to realize and learn the effects of love. Our daily decisions will associate with working towards one conclusion or another. One is to realize that the choices we make have to do with the lack of love and trying to get that feeling back, or the abundance and trying to keep it. What would it be like to let go of all the concepts, rules and past experiences you have of love and, instead, open your heart to feel the love from within, not to be driven by past love, good or bad, only to be driven by your inner present love? First, this love is achieved by recognizing and accepting that everything that presently exists was created or developed and presently loved by something or someone in the world. Second, you can only love others as much as you love yourself. When you struggle with others at school, work, or even at home, you are not struggling with them at all. You are actually struggling with yourself. As Deepak Chopra has said, "Every fault you see in them touches a denied weakness in yourself."

You can trace almost all domestic violence to the lack of love or having poor relationships, which started in either childhood or even in romantic relationships. I believe that all the people in the world who commit violent crimes or who are engaged in terrorism, at some point, experienced a deep lack of inner love. We don't want that path to be taken by our children. When a child knows his self-worth, no one can make him feel worthless. Well, how do we do that?

1. As an adult, **start displaying self-confidence and worth in yourself.** A child can't do it if he doesn't see it in the home or school.
2. Create children that are **school wise, street smart and home geniuses!** Spend time with your child to get him to understand that getting good grades in school is not his future. Absorb EVERYTHING the school has to offer; then apply it to the world which is in the streets and at home to create a legacy and a career.

3. Give a child **responsibilities** without financial rewards. The most satisfaction one can get is a sense of accomplishment.
4. **Monitor school influences.** You don't want anything or anyone to work against your positive work at home.
5. **Listen to the child.** Usually that requires you also to spend time sitting with the child. No radio. No T.V. Just alone time to listen. If you have a child who may not speak freely, make sure you ask questions that cannot be answered by only yes or no. Do not ever accept nonverbal responses like nodding and shoulder shrugs.
6. **Allow him to make mistakes.** Ask any truly successful person, and he will tell you that real lessons come from making mistakes. But don't leave your child in the mess. Have empathy, and encourage him to try again.
7. **Teach children refrain from limiting love to a few people and denying it to others.**

Let me elaborate on this seventh point with an extended analogy. We need to love each other the way we love an unborn baby. If you think about it, though we never see an unborn child, we just know it's there. Most people who never before went to the doctors, now go monthly. Mothers sometimes start eating better. Some who may have had the habit of smoking quit smoking. But most importantly, you love the child before you even see it. And then once the child is born, he is the most beautiful thing you've ever seen. Tell me now how do we love people we are predestined to meet in the future? How will we make strangers feel? Do we love them before we even see them? We know people are out there. Do we take care of ourselves? Do we change our eating and exercising habits in anticipation of the people we are going to meet because by making better life choices we will be able to serve someone we haven't even met yet? Then do we make the person, whom we have never seen before until that first day, just like a newborn, feel like they are the most precious thing on earth? Do we have the sense that we would do anything in the world for them? Do we greet them with a smile or a hug? How do we make them feel? Love is secretly spelled with another four-letter word: F-E-E-L. Feeling is one of the goals of love. Teach kids to respect people the way we treat newborn babies.

"Love...So many people use your name in vain...Love. Those who have faith in you sometimes go astray...Love. Through all the ups and downs the joys and hurts...Love. For better or worse I still will choose you first." Love can see what is invisible to the eye. Therefore, children must choose love first. Have kids approach it as the last round in a game of hokey pokey. In the last round what do you do? You put your whole body in So put your whole body in love and shake it all about. Turn yourself around . . . because that's what it's all about.

Today is a new day, so don't ruin a good day today because of a bad yesterday. Choose love from now on.

Choose to let go of old hindering feelings and limitations of love. Choose to embrace and love how you look. Stop focusing so much on how you look materialistically. Choose to forgive whoever you need to forgive to move forward. Choose making healthy relationships. Choose to not compare yourself to others. Choose your health. Choose at least one personal vacation a year. Choose to deliver what you deserve.

"Love is just a word.
What matters is the connection that it implies."

Rama Kandra, *The Matrix Reloaded*

HAVE

Other than oxygen, you don't need anything. O.K. Well, after two to three weeks you may need food and definitely water along the way. The word, "have," is defined as "to possess, own, or hold". It is crucial to teach our children that they do not have to "HAVE" a lot of things that they think they do in order to survive.

I was watching one of those news shows one time about an experiment where parents took cell phones from teenagers for only a weekend. You would have thought that they told some of these teens they only had two days to live. All the cries could be aided by, "But I have to have my phone!" "I don't know what's going on anywhere!" "I don't know what people are saying about me!" How did kids get that way in such a short period of time? Modern cell phones as we really know them have only been out since the mid 1990's. Barely a generation later, I've seen kids as young as three years old go ballistic over a device that they claim they had to have. But it's not just phones. There is a long list of other things, including electronic devices, food, toys or even places to visit. I think what makes it worse is that most parents don't see anything wrong in feeding children this behavior. I don't know how many times I've even heard parents say, "I need Mookie to be able to call me in case of an emergency." First of all, most students aren't allowed to have phones in their possession during school. High school students, maybe. Secondly, if something really seriously pops off, a child doesn't have time to grab a phone to call Mommy. He would be trying to get out of that dangerous situation.

Afterschool sports, arts, clubs etc. activities I can see. "Hey, Mom. Practice is over and I'll be outside the gym."..."Dance rehearsal ended early. Can you come get me?"

I can even see dual custody issues. Parents of a child don't communicate well, and the child may have a phone to talk to a parent independently.

Nevertheless, I will say that there are a few things that I would say as adults we must teach children that they must "have".

We teach children that they must "**have**" discipline and put past offenses behind them. Ironically, as I'm writing this chapter, I just finished watching the 2016 AFC wildcard game between the Pittsburgh Steelers and the Cincinnati Bengals. The Steelers won 16 – 15, but they should have lost. After the running back for Cincinnati, Jeremy Hill, fumbled the football with just 83 seconds away from a total clenching, and after a 15-yard penalty on Vontaze Burfict, who hit Antonio Brown of the Steelers in the head with his shoulder on an uncatchable ball with 18 seconds left in the game, the Steelers landed within field goal range.

Then, as the Steelers' medical staff tried to get Brown off the field, both teams stood near one another at about the Bengals' 35-yard line leading to another 15-yard dead ball flag and penalty on Adam Jones of the

Bengals. As most rival games and playoff games are in any sport, things had been getting heated more and more as the game went on. But because these two men playing in professional football were not able to put behind them previous plays and calls, their behavior cost their team, fans, fellow players and themselves, the game and the season and the chance to win the Super Bowl that year. How selfish! So you have to put the past behind you.

Sometimes you'll also see evidence of this behavior in teens or young adults who start to bully other kids or, worse, commit the crime of mass shootings. It usually starts that they were unable to put something from their past behind them in order to move on with their lives socially and emotionally. Now, of course, I'm not referring to any major traumatic events that may occur in a child's life like a sudden death, a natural disaster. These events will need additional psychological or spiritual guidance and direction to get them through. Other than these events children have to able to put the past events behind them.

We as adults must teach:

Children, **"have"** to learn to take care of themselves first (at least more than anyone else). Some people would initially think this is selfish, but my response to that is, unless you take of yourself first, you can't be any good to anyone else. One can't give not unless his basic needs are taken care of. So I'm not talking about teaching a child to make sure he has a Bugatti and a summer home with a live-in maid and chef before he does things for others.

But you do have to do what you need to do to keep your life in order.

Children **"have"** to say "thank you." The lesson here is that it is tough when a child is dealing with someone of authority, a teacher, boss, or family member who has probably had either tough love with him or even yelled at him. But at the end, in a calm voice, the child can say to the person in authority, "Well, OK. Thank you for your time." For a teenager, it's tempting for him to tell the adult exactly how he feels, or as a child to say, "I'm going to tell my mother." And depending on the situation, maybe he should, because a child shouldn't have to fight his battle if an adult is rude to him. But besides that, saying thank you and showing gratitude in all situations will take a child a long way.

Children **"have"** to eat well. Nothing else will matter if a child does not eat well and put the right foods in his body. All the money, success and accomplishments won't mean a thing if he is not healthy enough to enjoy them or see things through.

Children **"have"** to get plenty of sleep. Trying to operate and perform tired is as dangerous as, if not more than, trying to operate a vehicle drunk. One cannot be productive if he doesn't have adequate sleep. Also, lack of sleep is not good for one's health. Lack of sleep can lead to poor relationship building and even depression. This is dangerous because most would not link this to a lack of sleep. They would place blame on the external factors. Plus, organs in the body have to rest in order to function properly.

Children **"have"** to stop spending time with the wrong people. We're not saying children it is a must to stop hanging around all their old friends, but they need to spend more time with fellow peers who have a common, promising future and not a common past. Unfortunately, a lot of adults who have the power of hiring, writing letters of recommendation, making referrals will judge a child, most of the time, by the company he keeps. Not saying it's fair, but it is done. But here's the main thing. A person will always be the sum total of the people with whom he associates. If the people around with don't have what you want in life, then you need to limit, or maybe even totally remove yourself from, those people.

Children **"have"** to stop lying to themselves. In a lot of my seminars and workshops I'll ask the question, "What is the hardest thing in the world to do?" Answer: "To tell the truth about yourself." It is only in our true honesty that we will find our true reality. It's funny how we have more integrity with our family, work, and church. But we don't have integrity with ourselves. We can easily see it just on New Year's resolutions alone. We'll promise to start this. We'll promise to stop that. But before the year, if not month, is out, we've broken a promise. And the sad thing, maybe outside of your family, no one really cares or appreciates all the effort and integrity you showed them. At your funeral, if they show up, depending on the weather I'm sure, you'll get a few good words, though some false, and even fewer tears. But what will last far beyond the funeral and the good food at your repass? The legacy one has left to this world. We get only one shot at it. So children have to stop lying to themselves about who they really are. In a sense, they become their own biggest "bully". If this problem is not addressed, a child will lie, steal, abuse and cheat with more damage done to himself than any outside person or event can do.

"You can lie to yourself and the rest of the world, but your results will tell the absolute truth."

Larry Wingett

Children **"have"** to stop running from their problems. Though the imagination can be a child's biggest strength and asset, imagination can often be his biggest enemy. A child can turn a small issue into a great big problem, which he then fears, runs away from, and allows to grow into something which truly is an issue or problem. Yes, it sounds like adults we know, doesn't it? Well that's what I'm trying to avoid. When a child is afraid, he has given up his option to take positive action. Fear to face problems is the killer of initiative. It is the killer of action. At best you get re-action, and that is rarely the best thing for a child to do. By facing your problems, you push all that away from you.

When a person faces his problems, he can clear his head, make better choices, and take action. If a child does anything less, he will have a very difficult time overcoming his problems. If a child can face his fears, he may still have a difficult time, but at least now he will stand a chance in succeeding in life, and his fate is largely in his own hands and not the hands of anyone else.

Children **"have"** to stop looking to others for happiness, at least until he has the true definition. Most people, when they are seeking "happiness", are actually seeking "pleasure". Pleasures are those temporary things that kids and adults seek and are often mistaken for happiness: Toys. Cars. Games. Jewelry. Clothes. Food. Sex. Pleasures are anything that is marketed to us. It is what we use to numb our reality. Though the small previous list can sometimes have a high price tag, it is still cheaper than doing what we really need to do to obtain happiness.

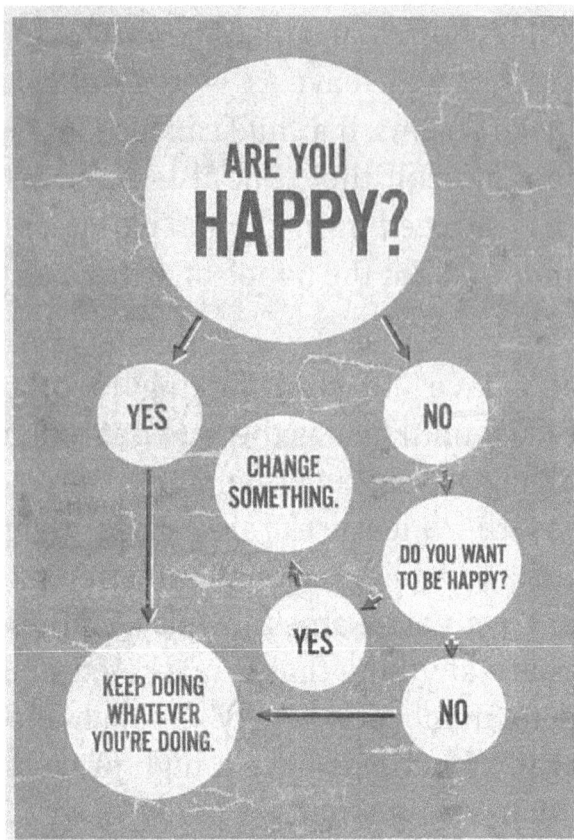

Now let's define happiness. Happiness is the process of identifying your ideal self. You can't find something that's already there. Happiness exists now. It's not something you have to find. That's like trying to find your breath.

It's the negative grasping of the mind that causes unhappiness. If you're not happy, it's because your mind doesn't allow you to be happy. And if your mind doesn't allow you to be happy, it is because of the choices that YOU are presently making in your life. It's not about what people do to you nor the past events that you have no control over; it's about what you choose to do after what people do to you or that event.

Other personal qualities that children must "**have**" include empathy, creativity, compassion, the desire to be a life-long learner, good listening skills, the awareness of when to be a good follower and leader, honesty, integrity and courage.

Courage is the last point on which I want to elaborate. A child has to be groomed to stop thinking that he or she is not ready for life's challenges because of age, size, color, or gender. Courage will give a child the power of balance and his favor in life. With control and power over aspects of one's life, a person will be able to see and recognize that the rewards that life has to offer out-weigh the risks. But he needs to "**have**" courage to do it.

When we think of super heroes on T.V. or in movies, we think of them as having courage. Most times we relate courage with being fearless and having physical strength. Though **physical** strength is one way of displaying courage, there are actually five other strengths that superheroes display courage in that have even more significance in their lives and ours too.

There's courage to confront **spiritual** issues. Salvation is one of the top topics that one has to face in his or her life. There are over 4,200 religions, faiths and spiritual beliefs. With so many people, doctrines and cultures in our spiritual society, it really takes courage to make what you feel to be the right choice. After all, we're not trying to decide between a brown or beige Kenneth Cole sweater from Marshals. We are talking about eternal life here. And the courage really comes if the choice you make is different from what your parents believe in.

There's courage to confront **social** issues. This is one of the biggest ones that children, especially teens, have to have courage to stand up to. Social courage will lead to success in any type of relationship that a child may desire. It will also have residual effects for financial growth through the powers of social networking.

There's the courage to confront **moral** issues. Children have to know when to stand up to what is right. Now in a school and home setting, there are proper procedures and a certain level of respect that has to be followed. Examples I see of this are on episodes of "Cops" or "The First 48." The criminals are always cocky and act big and bad...until they get caught. They begin to sputter stories between tears and sniffles about how they knew what they were doing was wrong. It was an accident. Their life took them down this path. In today's society, everyone has a camera and "big brother" has cameras everywhere. Heck. Kids themselves have cameras and denigrate themselves on social media. It is important to teach kids to always do the right thing. You never know who's watching.

There's the courage to confront **emotional** issues. Emotions are some of the most destructive conditions on earth. Every war, fight, murder was based on an emotion. On the contrary, some of the greatest creations have been made out of emotions too. You, for one. A lot of great humanitarian acts are engendered from emotions. But unfortunately, children fall short by frittering away their potential, focusing instead on the negative emotions. When we get upset, a lot of times we forget what was said to us, but how we were left feeling never leaves us. It takes courage to confront that emotion. But it is necessary. Hanging on to a negative emotion is like your soul being draped with an x-ray lead blanket. Yes, you can still function, but that weight is always there. And instead of confronting with courage, we cope, sometimes with self-imposed defeat.

Children are enthralled by superheroes. But no matter who the superheroes are, what are they most afraid of? Answer: Having their true identity discovered. .. which leads to the last point, to "**have**" courage to live the **truth**. And the irony, just like us in real life, the difference is only a matter of a mask, or a pair of glasses. The truth is never that far away. How far, physically, is Clark Kent from Superman? Peter Parker from Spiderman? Bruce Wayne from Batman?

Though all the other "haves" are extremely important, this one will make the others more fun, more productive and easier. If we can work with children to get them to understand that our whole society is built on overcoming fear. Look at the commercials. Most commercials deal with the fear of being without or scrutinized because others have, fear of not looking a certain way, fear of not having some type of security. The list goes on. Though this is very unfortunate for our society, it can provide a world of opportunities for our children. It is so obvious that people don't realize how important it is to be truthful to themselves. We have to understand that in the whole history of the world, there was never anyone like you and there never will be again. EVER!!! If we truly understood that, we would live differently. We would love differently, hate never, give more, and want less. Everyone would end his life having lived fully with no regrets. He would had been truthful about all his desires, directions and decisions. Disciplines would be easy. Procrastination ripped from the dictionary.

Teach the children to live their truth! Teach the children to have courage! Though it may be very lonely and challenging at times, it is the only way your creator expected you to live. By unnecessarily not living your fullest, you have a lot of explaining to do after your death. Good luck with that.

COURAGE!

WANT

So many times if you hear a child say, "I 'want' this...I want that..." 9.9 times out of 10 he is referring to some material object that he didn't earn, buy or have any idea what it may really take to obtain it financially or time wise. Now with the four-letter-word **WANT** with a child, one has to be careful in how to let a child know that one, not that they can't have what they see or desire, but is it something that they truly want? And two, if so, once it's in his possession, how is what he has going to benefit his growth, his relationships and or the universe?

There's nothing wrong with wanting things. The problem is that people will do or say whatever they need to get it. This is when kids lie or steal for the first time. They may have asked for it. You, as the responsible parent or adult, said, "No," and the next thing you know you see that same piece of candy at home.

"How did you get that?" you ask.

The kid shrugs his shoulder.

"What do you mean you don't know? Isn't that the same candy I told you that you couldn't have from the store?"

The kid shrugs his shoulders again.

"Mookie. Did you steal this candy?"

"But I really wanted it." He finally responds in his whinny voice.

Now lesson number one is possession. Of course as the responsible adult you'll talk about stealing and having to explain buying something with money. Lesson two. The lesson about getting into trouble for taking something that is not yours. Lesson three. How would you feel if someone took something from you without asking? Now after you get those out of the way or if your child is still young enough that you haven't had to go back for those lesson, there is the lesson of self-value and self-worth. I'm going to assume that you have already read my first book, so I don't have to go over all the power points. Just assure a child that he or she is no less deserving than any other person on this earth. All that this world has to offer is at his fingertips and they are deserving of every atom. However, the question should be asked, "Why do you want said item?"

Wanting can be good to sustain or even ignite a drive or fire to take action and the real reward is the journey you took to get there. Bad thing is that one can be doing it to prove someone wrong. You know the old saying, "Oh yeah. I'll show them." Then you'll spend 10 – 20 years on wanting something for the wrong reasons.

Let's look at the etymology of the word 'want'. Going back to the 1200th century, 'want' had the meaning of deficient and insufficient. Later on it had the attachment of shortage and poverty. If we are made in God's image, we are never deficient or short of anything. But the embedded and learned accepted mindset of "WANT" leads us to believe that we are lacking. Yes. We need to eat. We need to clothe ourselves, we need to exercise. We need to bathe. We need to love. But the 'wants' come from society's introduction and definition of what people want. George Washington never wanted a Maserati. Nefertiti never wanted shoes from Manolo Blahnik. So how can you give power to something that doesn't exist? Think about it. The world existed just fine before any of the products that people desire were even created. There shouldn't even be a 'want' in anyone's life. At least not the want of something that doesn't have a purpose of building, saving or creating. We have to reprogram and teach the children the definition of 'want'. Any want outside the want to build, recreate, encourage, motivate, love, salvage, or add goodness to this world can possibly lead to a selfish, greedy, undeserving, unnecessary, non-contributing, and destructive want. The positive 'want' should be paralleled with contentment and gratuitousness. A person should always be just as happy where he is as he journeys to where he is going. A person should be just as joyous with the trinkets that he has as well as he anticipates being with the ones desired in his mind.

Think back, if you can, when you were born. All you 'wanted' was to eat, sleep and be loved. Now think, and you probably don't have to think that deep. Isn't that all you really want to do now? Sure, a savory stuffed crab imperial may taste a lot better than some season-less porridge. But porridge is food. If you were hungry, and didn't have many choices, the porridge would be just fine. We as adults make efforts to introduce the "finer" things that the world has to offer without losing the appreciation of where we are and what we have presently. Also, as a child is being introduced to more things, simultaneously a child should be taught to give. The problem is that all we know, especially in Western civilizations is to receive, receive, receive. We are only taught to mandatorily give at Christmas, Birthdays, Valentine's Day, funerals, baby showers, bat mitzvahs and weddings. And as I found out at my own wedding, I see that some people didn't get that memo either. Now I know that we always have an answer for everything. "But you don't know where I came from. You don't know my circumstances." Or "You only live once, so I'm going to get all that I can."...But you have to release the desire to justify your actions. And I purposely used the word release because it is something that we are choosing to hold on to. It has nothing to do with family, cultural, job environment or circumstances. Every day that we live to want beyond what we really need is a choice. Choose, to 'want' healthily by always being content with what you have and as your desires grow give at least as much as you're growing or taking.

Now I know the details and the changing of the mindset is a lot more than just the few words that I have mentioned in this chapter. But let me help get you started with an example from just one of the biggest crises known to man. Sibling rivalry! Now this is based on the word 'want' in slightly a different direction. Usually it's in the form of, "I want my brother to die." "I wish my sister was never born." "I hate you." "I wish you would move out." "Go kill yourself." And this is the short list of comments that you have heard...or used yourself over the years. Regardless of your nationality, I'm sure that you'll appreciate the point I'm about to make.

It wasn't that long ago that many children were born into slavery in the United States. Remember, when the Constitution was originally written, it did not include slaves. Slaves were considered as 3/5 of a human. "We the people" did not include people of Spanish descent, Blacks, Asian descent or even the native Indians. As time went along on many plantations up and down the east coast for various reasons such as additional labor, breeding and sex slaves, many siblings were separated from their parents and many from each other; and, of course, not by choice. And it was not because they said something wrong to them or they were in their space. Purely for whatever gain for the next slave owner. Many times siblings could only stand by and watch as the new slave owner drove off over the horizon with their brother or sister to never be seen or heard from again. That's why it bothers me when I hear or see siblings arguing over small stuff. They may think that it's big, but if they were to look into the history of their culture, then whatever their sibling did is not really that big of a deal. Family was the biggest possession people had and to have that taken away from you with no choice! Those who were slaves 'wanted' to be together but couldn't. And here we are often wishing our siblings dead or gone. The miracle to be in existence with someone in close DNA to you is powerful. I always love to watch schools of fish swimming in sync. When one moves, all the others move. A beautiful thing. The same could be with humans. Of course, we have our own personality, but there is no reason why when one is happy, the others couldn't be happy. When one is successful, the others feel the success. When one grows, the others also rejoice in the growth. Think about the power of that in the world. Think of a flower. Does a flower look good with one petal? NO. At least two or more are needed to consider it a thing of beauty. And you won't see a daffodil win any spring floral awards with just one petal. Think about in our patriotic song, *America the Beautiful* and the verse, "amber waves of grain". One stalk in our hand is just usually a non-attractive tawny looking weed. But it takes acres of that same "grain" to create the amber beauty that made it into the song.

"An inheritance gained hastily in the beginning will not be blessed in the end."

Proverbs 20:21

The take home point for this chapter and to teach kids is this, they have to be aware that most things that people may "want" are things that they aren't willing to work for. Most of one's success in life comes from mastering the things that he doesn't do. You may have heard of the adage, "The greater the risk, the greater the reward." Children need to be taught and shown by adults that nothing great comes from those who sit around and wish. You can't just sit around and hope. James 2: 17- 18, "*17 So also faith by itself, if it does not have works, is dead.18 But someone will say, 'You have faith and I have works.' Show me your faith apart from your works, and I will show you my faith by my works."* Simple. Whatever a child may "want", has to be worked for. at least if he wants it to be of any good to society or for his life to be meaningful. Relationships. Have to be worked for.   Freedom. Has to be worked for. Health. Has to be worked for. Mastery of a skill. Has to be worked for.

But what if a child wants **happiness, peace, Joy, a balanced life, fulfillment, confidence or stability?** Well. They already possess all these things. We have to teach and work with children to work on what's inside. All of these children can have every single day if they choose to have them. If any of the listed items are missing, it's not because they are not there, it's because of an emotional reaction that one chooses to have to a particular event. For example, when it snows, some people get upset. The streets and sidewalks are bad, kids are home from school, snow has to be shoveled from around the cars. But in the same snow storm, retailers can sell extra coats and gloves. A lot of people make extra money plowing and shoveling. Ski resorts can make money. Same event but different reactions. The example I like to use a lot comes from my being a firefighter. Though I am a firefighter, I don't care for call to put out fires too much. I became a firefighter for the rescues. But of course I can't pick or choose my calls. Nevertheless, if a car is flipped over on the highway, for most, this is a tragic event. Bodily injury. Property damage. For me, and for others in the fire and EMS department, police department, and hospitals, this is an opportunity for us to do what we enjoy doing. Same event, different reactions.

Nevertheless, the end result of our "want" is in the mind of each individual. Obviously, all that I "want" isn't what anyone else would want. And what everyone else wants is not what I want. When working with children, we must make sure that what they "want" is not only what they truly want, but it is what they want and not what the family, society, government, friends, trends and the media want. And be careful of most religious groups and organizations as well. I was recently watching a video online where in order to show your faith, the members of this one church had to eat the heads of rats and snakes...

Also, we have to accept that it is possible that no matter how much we may work to get something that we "want," it just may not happen in our time and understanding but in God's time and of power far beyond our understanding. So many times in my life, I did the goal thing, and I just knew without a doubt that I wanted a particular thing, status or goal. I would have taken it to the bank. But I would say at least 90% of the time, not only what I set out for didn't happen, but what did happen when it was all said and done was even better than what I thought I wanted. God and the Universe know what you want better than you do. So it is important that we teach our children to not set their desires on what they want, but to put more focus on the journey being just a little bit better than the day before each and every day. And wherever you are, be there. Enjoy the moment. Here's the secret of this whole chapter. I've never known anyone to totally achieve what they "want". For example, an athlete or a minister, let's say, may be content with their career at the end...But they are constantly improving their craft to be victorious. No one ever achieves all that he wants. Even if everything you mapped out came out perfect, and, let's say, your goal was to get all of that by the age of forty, and you did it by the age of thirty-nine. Still by that time you would have acquired new goals and a new set of wants. It never ends, my friends...It never ends. That is just part of human nature.

"Success isn't about just what you accomplish in your life, but it's what you inspired others to do."

Author Unknown

"A strong, successful man is not a victim of his environment. He creates favorable conditions. His own inherent force and energy compel things to turn out as he desires."

Orison Swett Marden

READ

Anyone who knows me knows these two things about me. One, I love *Star Wars*. Two, I love Snoopy. To give a tribute to Charles Schultz, anytime I write or if it fits in on any speech of mine, like in my Toast Masters Chapter, I always try to start my book or speech with, "It was a dark and stormy night..." And this love for Snoopy came from my reading the Sunday paper. (For you young folks out there: The Sunday paper is a very much slower hard copy version of the Internet. The news, sports, fashion, advertisements, and entertainment came once a week in paper form.) I was excited to receive the Sunday paper every week. Charles Schultz and other comic strip writers kept us not only laughing but informed with what was going on in the world. Comics allowed you to see other cultures, use your imagination, use analytical thinking. But by and far it taught me how to read. Words I didn't know I looked up in the dictionary...or I would ask my mother, full time human dictionary, part-time English teacher. A child's goal should be to read more because reading is a valuable way of self-educating themselves. Children are fed stories and information when they are younger; but sadly, as they become adults, they far too often neglect one of the most important tools in life. Most people after high school or college only read because they have to, not because they want to, not realizing that they always have to. The world is changing too fast not to read something all the time. Reading is the best way to improve your mind. If you want to get smart and stay smart so you can have the edge over the average person, you need to learn new things. Reading is one of the best ways to learn and expand your knowledge.

Reading is one of the cheapest forms of entertainment; it is even free on the internet or in libraries. To get a child to start reading, it is better to get him to read books of his or her interest. The key: read with him. A child will always run across words he doesn't know. You need to be by his side to help him through. You have to make a child feel it's okay to stumble through reading. They'll get it eventually. I always encourage children to always have a dictionary nearby and don't be afraid to use it. And this should start very early in a child's life. After a couple of years, a child should read a variety of books to suit his preferences including fiction books, educational, mysteries and suspense thrillers, science fiction, history, sports, music, and health related articles because reading is a great way to feed the mind and spirit. When you don't stimulate the mind with information or engross it in a compelling and captivating stories, you are paving the way to boredom and a mundane life.

Because the human mind is a never-ending processing machine that is always seeking information. Reading will help to nourish and stimulate a child's mind and keep it engaged, diverting his mind from negative thinking and worrying. Keeping good reading material in front a of child will balance out the negative influences. It would be very advantageous too if you can actively seek friends that have the same interest in reading. That way, they'll see that it's acceptable amongst his peers to read at his age.

A lot times we are shuttling kids back and forth. Keep books in the car. And the key here is to keep the radio off. A car ride should be time to either talk to your child or let him read. PERIOD. Nothing else. No phone for you. No games. No movies. A child's brain is always seeking information. If you don't provide what you want for him, the world will.

Share with kids these following points to make reading a must in his life:

1) Reading can calm a child if he is bothered or upset.

If a child reads on a regular basis, reading can help him to relax and quiet his mind which in turn can help him reduce his stress levels. Burying into a book is a great way of taking his focus of attention off his troubles and worries for a while as it transports him to seemingly better places of imagination and fantasy worlds. A Book can take a child out of his world and away from his personal perspectives and difficulties. In fact, reading has such a powerful influence it can change a child's emotional state. Stories of inspiration can motivate and inspire a child while happy stories can improve a child's mood.

2) Reading can improve a child's quality of conversations.

A child's vast array of knowledge will help him to become more involved in discussions, he will be more able to instigate much more variable and interesting levels of conversations. Obtaining more information will give a child a distinct advantage over other children because he would have gathered a much wider understanding of many subjects and topics of conversation. There's nothing like a well-rounded person. People will only want to do business with someone they trust. And if you sound knowledgeable, then you can potentially be trusted. Limited knowledge can seriously hold a child back and leave him feeling left out in some social situations. Limited knowledge also could lead to insecurity, self-doubt, and lack of confidence. Ultimately, this will make a child feel very much more interesting and refreshing of a child to be around.

Most parents underestimate the power gained from a child reading which can be priceless. Reading expands a child's knowledge and awareness. Reading will also stimulate his creative imagination.

3) Reading engages a child's imagination.

Story books can engage a child in a world which is miles apart from his own world. This could be calming or even therapeutic. A child can have a glimpse of what goes on in the lives of many fictional characters. Then this vicarious experience can have the potential to spark positive ideas of what can transpire in his own in reality and create something positive for the community.

When a child engages a curious mind into a book he can experience empathy, sympathy and compassion with the characters. A child can travel anywhere in a book and he is allowed to meet and engage in an author's fantasy world. Fiction books will allow a child to use his own imagination to paint his own version of the images, characters, and places. Every book can give a different representation of the characters and the location to each reader because every child's imagination will perceive things slightly differently.

4) All leaders and successful people read.

Unfortunately, there's a saying out there amongst the wealthy..."If you want to hide the secret to success from the lower class, put it in a book." Leaders are readers. We have to embed into children's minds that books are very powerful. They change and transform lives. Nearly all successful people will tell you that there is at least one book that they read that completely turned around and transformed their life. Children must know and believe that information and knowledge can mean power. It can lead to inspiration and success. But one of the main things I've noticed about leaders in the world is that they all have good stories to tell. Therefore, you have two choices as a leader. Either go out and live your life so you will have your own stories, or read plenty of books to share other people's story. The mind loves a good story. We are told stories from the moment we are born. Stories are powerful ways of influencing the subconscious mind. The next time you go to church, pay attention to the audience. Most people are "listening," but they perk up a little more when the minister or pastor starts telling a story. Look at Joel Osteen, a very successful and renowned T.V. evangelist, author and minister. In a 30-minute sermon, he could tell anywhere from three to six stories. He even opens up his sermons with a story or joke. Some stories from books will inspire you. Reading then sharing stories about other people's success or how they overcame seemingly impossible feats which required immense courage and determination can give your audience great inspiration to go on and achieve their dreams, believing that if other people have already done it, then they can too. And as the presenter, you delivered that hope or spark because you initially read it in a book and all you did was share it.

5) Reading a book can improve a child's health.

A lot of teens find that reading can help them unwind and relax at night. It can help them to drift off to sleep easily because you're leaving behind your troubles of the day as you allow your immersion in your book to relax you.

Frequent reading helps improve a child's concentration, and this helps to exercise and boost a child's memory power because it encourages him to remember details, main ideas, characters and facts. The mind is like the body; it needs exercising just like your muscles do. Once you engage yourself in a good book, your focus will shift from your troubles as you become oblivious to what's happening in the outside world.

Other benefits of reading deal with a child's emotional well-being and physical health. When a child worries or experiences periods of anxiety, he can get trapped emotionally inside his head. Reading will shift focus away from his troubles and concerns. When his attention goes onto the book or article he is reading, he can begin to relax his mind and body and give himself some much-needed rest and energize himself for the next school day or whatever tasks that may be ahead.

We spend our younger years in school, anxious to graduate. We think that school is so tough. We believe that school is "the Man" holding us down. We are trapped in what seems like this never-ending vortex of rules, time obligations, tasks and assignments. Sentenced to 13 – 18 years of school! Then graduation. We are free! On the contrary, this is the time when we become the true prisoners. We stop reading. We stop learning. Now we are prisoners for the next 40 – 60 years of the opinions, rules, commands and directions of politics, your boss, and society. When we stop reading and learning for ourselves we are at the mercy of the environment around us. The true rulers of our world are those who never stop reading. Those who make the decisions, those who hold the reins of our future, those who weave the fabric of society, all are continual learners and readers. Therefore, if you choose to no longer read and learn after graduation, then your prison sentence actually starts after graduation from high school or college. The freedom we were looking for was with us all along. We give up our freedom the moment we stop learning. Freedom cannot exist if the one who seeks freedom no longer moves. The etymology of freedom comes from the 14th century Middle English and breaks down into the root word "free" and the suffix "dom" which means condition of status. Around the 16th

Century it took on the meaning of "possession of particular privileges." If you want possession of particular privileges, stopping your education isn't the answer. On the contrary, your formal education is just the foundation, the beginning of your true education. Traditional education is okay for the basics math, phonetics, social skills, history, the arts, science. And it's basic because, by law, at least in the United States, it has to be offered for free to every child. Once you're done with the basics, you can continue your quest for freedom by focusing on and specializing in what you really want to do with your life. You can focus on your contribution to the world. We are all magnificent creatures. We daily get more than we deserve, and we are capable of more than what we are daily achieving. In a lot of my seminars I try to put some perspective to our lives. Our choices need to be with the realization that in the history of the world, there was never anyone like you and there will never be another you. EVER. Therefore, we need to live our lives and continue to live with freedom, by our free will and not the will of a wanton society. But by not continuing to read and educate ourselves, we fall into the vortex of what others are accomplishing and not what our inner potential can contribute to this universe. True freedom arises when we are not dependent on something outside ourselves for the way we feel about ourselves.

Reading is significant! Everybody who wants his child or student to have a better life should be non-negotiable about reading at least one book every week. When we stop learning, we stop growing; and in this life you do one of two things: you either move forward in life or you stay where you are. Most people end up living their life in a kind of ground hog day. They think mostly the same old unhelpful thoughts day in and day out because their mind has nothing better to focus on. You cannot succeed in life with limited knowledge and information. If you want to expand your consciousness and your awareness of reality, then reading is still the best way of achieving this. Books can cover a more in depth look and wider scope into topics, as they can delve much deeper into a subject than any television documentary does. A film is often a shortened version of a book. The benefits of reading are limitless and it is an aged old tradition and past time which will never become outdated. With the technological revolution forever gathering pace, many people now overlook the benefits of reading.

Children: Read! If you don't know all of what's possible, you will not push your boundaries; and if you're not aware of what you are capable of, you're not going to achieve your true potential.

"It is what you read when you don't have to that determines what you will be when you can't help it."

Oscar Wilde

"The only important thing in a book, is the meaning that is in it for you."

W. Somerset Maugham

"What you don't know would make a great book."

Sydney Smith

"Once you learn to read, you will forever be free."

Frederick Douglas

GOAL

Okay. Let's get this out right in the beginning. If you're an adult reading this, setting a goal is only for children. As an adult your four-letter word is "done". As in, "get it done." Adults' two biggest problems are procrastination and making emotional decisions based on others' lifestyles and opinions. Really? Your emotional responses to others and living based on other's opinion is more important than you truly want in life. The people that make you angry, talk about you, you complain about truly determine your lifestyle. Before you laugh, or worse, deny what I'm saying, think back to when you were a child. Think about the car you said you wanted to drive, the house you wanted, the places you wanted to travel, the number of days you didn't want to work, what you really wanted to go to college for and or do for a living. Exactly. So yes, you do live your life based on others. You may even say, "But you don't know the boss I work for." You may complain about your job and boss, but you chose the job in the first place, and even worse, you choose to go back every day. Therefore, your four-letter word is "done". In the words of Larry Winget, in his book *Shut Up. Stop Whining and Get a Life!*: "Do what you have to do. Get it "done" and move on with your tasks."

As a child and young teen, a goal is good because it sets the mind to not only start processing organization, but also to have vision and focus. So by starting at an early age, setting a goal for a child immediately taps into his strength of vision and helps to sharpen it. Now what is the child going to "see"? Whatever they want and whatever you expose them to. A child already has great imagination at that age and believes whatever the parent tells them. Think of a child as a car. The engine is the child's imagination and the gas is the mental, social, physical and emotional fuel you as the adult choose to put inside of the engine. Now will the child/car run on regular gas? Well, yes, sure. But won't the imagination run better on the super high tech gas? Well yes, sure. Give a child short easy goals...Don't get a two year old to solve the antiderivative of 3 times the cosecant squared over pi. It's very important that you give a child goals that will one, show that you are supportive of them, and two, goals that will boost his self-confidence.

As a parent...teacher...or provider, a goal for a child is good when you want to mold a specific outcome or teach a particular life principle. A goal has to be SMART (Specific, Measurable, Attainable, Realistic, Timely) for a child. This means that though working with a child, you never know what's going to come out of his mouth or what imaginative conclusion he will come up with, but you should have some idea of a possible desirable outcome. A goal should never be used as punishment or based on threats.

Setting a goal will teach the valuable lesson of accountability. This is huge. Boys always have a lot to say and are so brash and confident until they get caught doing something they have no business doing. They often know from the beginning that they were wrong; and actually, the more times they get away with something, the brasher they get. But when caught, they either get mad, go into a state of denial, or cry like a baby. Girls have a tendency to stay in a state of denial or show minor signs of depression for the situations in which they often put themselves. This can be either with social events or even dating. Having a child learn accountability is important. It teaches him about sticking to his word and honoring his commitments, even if it means making a personal sacrifice or going that extra mile. It's beyond just being reliable. It's a child, and later an adult, that can be counted on to do the right thing even in challenging circumstances. It is also about being prepared to take responsibility for his actions and outcomes even when things go wrong. There's no pointing the finger to another student, parent or teacher. Nor can he blame circumstances or make excuses such as "I didn't have enough resources such as time or money." It's about taking ownership, and if need be, admitting a mistake and moving on to keep the school project, house responsibility, or whatever on track.

Setting a goal helps a child with problem solving. I don't know how many "young people" I've seen in horror and panic because they didn't know what to do when their computer died, GPS wouldn't work, car broke down, cell phone battery died, microwave goes up … the list goes on and on. Problem solving for a child is an essential skill. It provides the framework for continual improvement.

But the mistake that most people make for themselves is that their goal is not the end result. One would say, "At the end of next year I will...or "In the next five years I will be..." That is not the approach at all. Yes, you should know what your end result will look like, but after you map it out, your end goal is only the first. Your goal is the first thing in front of you. If you just zero in on that, before you know it, you will have accomplished the overall goal. Only solve the problem that is before you. That is the only true moment in time you have anyway.

Goal setting should encourage a rise in unethical behavior. This is something you have to be cautious of and watch in a child. Achieving a goal is not as important as a child wanting to please adults, especially parent. The desire to please adults is so high they will sometimes do things unethical to make the adult happy. This is the opportunity to let them know that integrity should be at the top of their list more than trying to make an adult happy. It's O.K. to fall short temporarily because ultimately there's always a lesson in the failure. It's part of the journey and failure is often the better lesson and reward than the success.

Setting a goal is good for balance. While a person is trying to achieve a goal, usually other daily responsibilities will be neglected. So, it is a good practice for a child to set his mind towards something specific and still take care of what needs to be done in other parts of his life.

Problem identification. While achieving a goal, a child can learn the difference between what's happening as part of the process or is there a potential problem to solve and take care of. A very important skill to develop in life. Also, a child needs to know the difference between something that is a big deal or a small deal. Emotional responses to events is huge in navigating potential setbacks in goals. I remember numerous times as a child I would do something wrong. I just knew it was lights out. Old school people, the kind where you got a beaten from your mother; then it was still the "and wait till your father gets home" threat that followed. But I don't know how many times my mother made me feel that it was okay. What I often thought was a big deal really wasn't; then I could move on mentally and physically with the task. Now that I think about it, nothing was ever a big deal. One time I think I got in trouble because I lied about something in school, maybe a report card or something; and I said to my mother, "A small thing, right, Mom?"

"No. That's a medium thing," she replied. . .with "the look."

I wasn't expecting that.

Make a decision. There are so many wishy washy and indecisive people in this world. After a child sets a goal, then he'll have to make a series of decisions to achieve that goal. So many children don't make the right decisions; but a lot of times, as in this case, *It's Not the Kids; It's the Parents.* The parents' patience and guidance will enable them and make good decisions. Parents are so afraid of Little Mookie's getting hurt, that the child never learns and strengthens the skill of making a decision and living with it. As the adult, you won't let them make any obvious life or death decisions. But for heaven's sake, let them decide on something.

Once a little boy was playing outdoors and found a fascinating caterpillar. He carefully picked it up and took it home to show his mother. He asked his mother if he could keep it, and she said he could if he would take good care of it.

The little boy got a large jar from his mother and put plants to eat, and a stick to climb on, in the jar. Every day he watched the caterpillar and brought it new plants to eat.

One day the caterpillar climbed up the stick and started acting strangely. The boy worriedly called his mother who came and understood that the caterpillar was creating a cocoon. The mother explained to the boy how the caterpillar was going to go through a metamorphosis and become a butterfly.

The little boy was thrilled to hear about the changes his caterpillar would go through. He watched every day,

waiting for the butterfly to emerge. One day it happened,
a small hole appeared in the cocoon and the butterfly
started to struggle to come out.

At first the boy was excited, but soon he became concerned.
The butterfly was struggling so hard to get out!
It looked like it couldn't break free! It looked desperate!
It looked like it was making no progress!

The boy was so concerned he decided to help.
He ran to get scissors, and then walked back
(because he had learned not to run with scissors...).
He snipped the cocoon to make the hole bigger
and the butterfly quickly emerged!

As the butterfly came out the boy was surprised.
It had a swollen body and small, shriveled wings.
He continued to watch the butterfly expecting that,
at any moment, the wings would dry out,
enlarge and expand to support the swollen body.
He knew that in time the body would shrink and
the butterfly's wings would expand.

But neither happened!

The butterfly spent the rest of its life crawling around with a swollen body and shriveled wings.

It never was able to fly...

As the boy tried to figure out what had gone wrong, his mother took him to talk to a scientist from a local college. He learned that the butterfly was SUPPOSED to struggle. In fact, the butterfly's struggle to push its way through the tiny opening of the cocoon pushes the fluid out of its body and into its wings. Without the struggle, the butterfly would never, ever fly. The boy's good intentions hurt the butterfly.

As a child goes through school, and life, keep in mind that struggling is an important part of any growth experience. In fact, it is the struggle that causes you to develop your ability to fly in life. Think about when you go to the gym to build muscle. It is only through the initial breaking down of the muscle and struggle that ultimately leads to the growth of the muscle.

Parents, I know it is hard watching someone you care about struggle. It could be a child grappling with homework, a project or practice for an upcoming recital. But while it is instinctive to want to help (and we often do by giving unsolicited advice), sometimes we need to learn to wait and let the process unfold on its own. We can watch and be there should any help be required, yet not intervene when there is no real need to.

The best thing you can do as an adult is set a desirable environment...Set an environment to set the goal. Set up opportunities for a child to get different experiences in life. Set a good environment for if the child fails. And probably the most important, set an environment for your child to get right back out there and try again and set another goal whether he succeeded or failed.

QUIT

I recently read an article about John Baird. In January of 1926, Mr. Baird invented the first mechanical "televisor" or television. Ironically, the screen was only 2" by 3 ½ ". About the same size as most cell phones. Keep in mind the major source of entertainment and news was delivered to people by way of radio up to this point. He was chastised and ridiculed severely for his invention which was made initially out of mainly household products. When trying to get publicity for his invention he went to the *Daily Press*. The editor was quoted, "For God's sake, go down to the reception and get rid of a lunatic who's down there. He says he's got a machine for seeing wireless. Watch him. He may have a razor on him." A reporter from *The Times* was quoted, "It has yet to be seen what extent further developments will carry Mr. Baird's system towards practical use." Well, two years after the introduction of his invention Mr. Baird introduced color television. By 1950, 9% of the United States had a television in the home. In 1954, the first coast-to-coast program, The Rose Bowl, was broadcast. On the 20th of July, 1969, 720 million people watched live the moon landing. Fast forward to today and Mr. Baird's "impractical" system has now turned up in 1.6 billion homes worldwide!

The point: Don't quit. It's very important to teach a child to complete and follow through with tasks, projects and commitments. I would say that no matter to you how outlandish a child's dream may sound and be in our adult understanding, support the child anyway. A child's mind is not tainted with doubts and fears. Adults birthed those traits. Though we want to positively influence our children, we have to make a conscious decision to not do it with our misaligned thinking.

In America, 73 percent of children begin playing a sport or instrument. About 55% quit before they turn 13. Why is this? Is this a good thing? Is it healthy? Is this damaging to a child's future?

Quitting is making us less human generation by generation. Quitting is becoming more of an instinctive trait than a choice. Any behavior is instinctive if it is performed without being based upon prior experience (that is, in the absence of learning) Sea turtles, as soon as they're hatched on a beach, will automatically move toward the ocean. A joey climbs into its mother's pouch upon being born. Many species of birds, without any thought, fly to southern climates for winter. If you accidently step on an ant hill, in an instant they will begin to rebuild the mound. And there are other examples that include animal fighting, animal courtship behavior, internal escape functions, and the building of nests. Yes, we are mammals. So, technically, we are animals. However, our brain is developed so we have what no other animal clearly has...the freedom of choice. But unfortunately, people and kids quit so easily in everything, it's becoming a normal and acceptable human trait and not a choice. Even in my after-school program when a student is getting ready to lose on a video game, he will restart the game before he will put any effort in figuring out how to solve the problem.

So why do children quit activities and tasks so easily? They quit because they can! Or at least we let them. Children are creating a pattern of quitting that is being supported by their parents mainly. Most of the time, adults are just too overprotective or too easily swayed by a child's attempt to get out of fulfilling his promises. I hear it all the time. "I'm tired." "It's too hot." "It's too cold." When you hear a child complain, "I have too much homework to do," then you know he wants to quit. It is easier to allow children to quit something than to make them stick it out until the end. Children learn an adult's soft spot early in life and will use it to get what they want. This includes quitting a home assignment they have started. If they see that they can quit without consequence, then they will learn this as a fact and quit whatever feels uncomfortable, challenging, frustrating, or boring to them as they develop and become teens and adults. It may not seem like a big deal when they are seven years old, but it certainly becomes a big deal when they want to quit their first job. Quit on their marriage. Quit on taking care of their children! Quit on their responsibility to the morals of their community or even the world. So let's set positive patterns now so that they learn commitment and the benefits of seeing goals and promises through to the end. Parents and adults, we need to help kids to face, sometimes, doing things they don't want to do. And because of the love of not seeing any child suffer in any fashion, we usually give in quickly.

For most children who start any activity, there's a honeymoon period when they are excited and anxious to play at every opportunity. But in about 75% of the cases, kids start to have feelings about their activity. If a child feels overwhelmed or under-challenged, he will want to quit. After all, when something is too difficult or too easy, it isn't fun anymore! The over-challenged child may feel as though he cannot keep up, catch up, or otherwise progress at the pace that the other children in sport, band or school assignment are progressing. The under challenged child will feel compelled to quit out of boredom or lack of follow up support from home to challenge the child. A child would have to possess a lot of self-love or motivation for the topic in order to continue without any nudging from an exterior source.

I remembered when I was in the 4th grade, there were many nights I spent listening to my father play his drum set in the living room. It was gold in color with silver sparkles. He would often play along with high speed jazz sets on LP records. [For you young people out there: An LP stands for Long Playing record or album. It defined the longer length of a particular song, unlike a "45" which was just a single song usually 3 – 5 minutes in length.] Well, I'm a big *Star Wars* fan. To this day, I don't know the name of the group or song, but my dad was playing a jazz song that had the *Star Wars* theme at the top of the piece. In the song was this great trumpet solo. I loved *Star Wars* so much, I immediately asked my mother for a trumpet so I could learn the instrument to learn the solo. She bought the trumpet. I didn't even take lessons other than the lesson my band director offered at school. I had at least two music books at home and taught myself how to play trumpet. In no time at all, I was playing first trumpet in band, often battling for first chair. Ever once in a while, I would play what I thought was a close version of the jazz solo to my dad. Though I thought I was close after six months, I remember my dad's chuckle and sarcastic agreement in my progress. (In 4th grade, I obviously didn't recognize sarcasm.) A year later, I remember saying to my dad, "I'll have this trumpet solo down in no time!"

"Trumpet solo?" My dad responded. "That's a saxophone."

My heart just fell. Plunged deep into the opaque musical composition of my soul. What did I do? I spent a whole year learning an instrument that I didn't need to learn. Even worse, I'm a whole year behind learning my Star Wars solo. Do I QUIT? I did what any logical 4th grader would do...I asked my mother if I could play the saxophone now...That was until my mom gave me "the look"...Old School! You know "the look". The look said, "Boy, don't even try it! I have only two months remaining on the 'rent-to-own-trumpet' and if you ask me to take this...(You can fill in your own 4-letter word here)...trumpet back now, I'll smack your mouth so hard, you'll have to pull your socks down to eat". That was what "the look" said; she never spoke a word. Needless to say, I kept playing the trumpet. But here's my point to this childhood story. I didn't want to quit learning how to play the song; I wanted to "quit" the instrument I had chosen to get to my goal. So, as you work with children and the idea of quitting, consider the following questions and thoughts:

1) The first question to ask is, "Who wanted to play the instrument or sport to begin with? The parent or the child?" When our children are young, they have little say in what activity they want to participate in. Usually, the choice is a matter of convenience for the parent. The practices, games or performances are nearby or at a local school or Recreation Center. Other children in the family or in the neighborhood friends participate in the same activity. Perhaps, the parent chose the activity, mainly sports, because he or she participated as a youth and wants the child to have the same positive experiences. A lot of times the parent, mainly fathers, want to relive their "glory days" through their child. The All City Al Bundy, Parent. "I served my country. I made four touch downs in a single game at my high school, Polk High." Possibly, the parent is still active in the sport and sees this as an opportunity to train with the child and spend quality time together. These are all inspiring and valid reasons for initially choosing a sport for your child. The issue, then, arises when the child is old enough (or willful enough) to undermine our best intentions as a parent, where is the balance of quitting, supporting, nudging, and encouraging?

2) If a child quits on the process, he is also quitting on the results. It is ludicrous to think that anyone anywhere will achieve anything by constantly quitting. It reminds me of the analogy of pumping a well on a country farm. When you start to pump the well, there is no water. You are actually priming the pump. If you were to stop pumping the well, the water would never rise to the top. It's the same principle with starting a worthwhile project in life. Though the line may not be straight, and may even be bumpy, dirty and all knotted up, the line is still connected and will still get you to the other end if you don't quit.

3) Once a child quits once, he'll start to set a pattern or habit of quitting. Everything in life, good or bad, once it's done once, it becomes easier every time. Work with your child to not make a habit of quitting. But as always, your child has to see or know that you didn't quit in anything either. Kids, especially teens, are quick to throw back at you, "Well you quit. Why can't I?" And hopefully that conversation isn't referring to you quitting on your own dreams.

4) Eliminating or minimizing quitting in a child helps him or her to become responsible for choices made. Besides the fact that taking responsibility for your choices shows great integrity for someone to own up to his mistakes, a child will, on the other hand, make better choices to begin with so he won't have to publicly take responsibility in the first place. If a child never has to take ownership for anything, he can just quit, quit,

quit. No big deal. They don't have to answer to anybody about any of their decisions.

Quitting is only for those who are doubtful of their outcome. We need to help children to be confident in their choices. Let them know that they are perfect in who they are presently and in whatever they decide to be in the future. I've noticed with athletes, successful movie stars and business professionals that it doesn't matter what material items they possess, it's a combination of their swagger and confidence and persistence that puts them on top.

You can't quit something that has existed before you. What do I mean? When you quit, what are you really quitting? You're not quitting on the activity. You are quitting on love, empathy, service, fearlessness, optimism, passion, acceptance, vision, purpose, generosity, joy, kindness, and ingenuity. All of these are what one is ultimately wanting to achieve. The activities that any one choses is just the means to arrive at any or all of these intangible goals. Since the beginning of Man, all of these intangible properties existed. It was just a matter of doing whatever we needed to do to see and or possess them. When one quits on any activity, especially without true merit, he is quitting on maximizing or obtaining what life is truly all about and all it has to offer. Therefore, you can't quit something that has existed before you were even born. It's up to us to find it within ourselves, be good stewards of it, and train others to find it themselves.

Instead of looking at situations as quitting, just think of it as changing the rules. Don't even think about it as looking "outside the box." What if you're supposed to look inside a trapezoid? Beneath an octagon? Or through a prism? Constancy, commitment and loyalty are all values we should hope to instill in children. Observe what the children are good at and what they are struggling with. Pay attention to their individual learning styles: Are they visual, auditory or kinesthetic (movement-oriented) learners? Build on their strengths. A lot of times kids want to quit because a parent is not there for them to either show off for or just to say, "I'm proud of you." If you can't show up to the games, theatre performances, concerts and a few sports practices, then you may not want to sign your child up. If you're a coach, mentor, or teacher and you're really doing it for the extra money, you may want to pass and get a part time job somewhere else. If you are in it for the right reason, parents and coaches and teachers need to stay in constant communication.

Bottom line: Learning not to quit in the world comes from learning not to quit through interactive activities and support at home. But I know this is easier said than done. If your kid wants to quit, let him quit but with an understanding or a consequence. And you may want him to reread the PAIN chapter of this book. Nothing beyond yourself will set you free. Focus on what truly matters to you and stick with it to the end. No matter what, don't quit!

SELF

This four-letter word, also, could have very easily been the title of the book. Our whole life awareness is based on how we view ourselves and/or how we feel about ourselves after someone else's opinion about us has been shared. You noticed that I said "life awareness." What does that mean? Children at a young age, do they care about an adult emotion or response? There could be a room of 1,000 people, and a child can be told that someone in this room has your toy. All you have to do is ask for it. What will the child do?

"Person #1, do you have my toy?"

"No."

"Person #2, do you have my toy?"

"No."

"Person #3, do you have my toy?"

"No."

And this child will go on and on until he or she finds the person in the room with the toy. The child doesn't care if he's in his diaper, pajamas, or Sunday suit. He wants his toy. The child doesn't care if people are in shock, appalled, helping him or laughing at him. The child doesn't care if only his friends or family in the room see him or if CNN is broadcasting it live all over the world. The child does not have "life awareness" yet, that is, not life awareness as we know it. At birth, he is given everything he needs, and then family, society, and environment slowly euthanize the child psychologically until it affects him physically. The way a child would approach trying to get his toy back is the way adults should approach life. Being an "adult" is supposed to be the ultimate stage of development, yet everything we want to achieve or can achieve in life is either delayed and or devoured by either no action because of concern of others' opinions or worries about how we will be viewed by others.

Dictionary.com defines "SELF" as "a person or thing referred to with respect to complete individuality." Complete. Individual. A child loses his complete individuality when he seeks his sense of self-worth from others. When it becomes very important to a child how others view him, his sense of value and self-worth and his confidence are dependent on external factors such as physical appearance, success, status, money, and fame. Then a child could start to seek praise from others. Though we see this in boys, we see this a lot in young girls. It's normal for a child to test her boundaries, but when a child starts to lose her sense of self, she will start doing things that she knows she'll get in trouble for or things to get attention, or things to help her to forget or even escape the realization of losing the battle of completeness and individuality. An affluent adolescent will spend too much of his parents' money. A child may even become promiscuous when he loses his completeness and individuality. This next one is big for younger children though older ones do this as well: getting angry for no reason at classmates and teachers. A younger child may do this because he doesn't know quite yet how to verbally communicate how he feels. This is where an imaginary friend may come in, to fix or fill the void or talking to voices that only he can hear. Nevertheless, these are all possible signs of a child trying to cope in losing his self. His completeness and individuality are being washed away.

When one starts to lose that **self** of who he is or meant to be, he is also losing that level of comfort which leads to a lack of confidence. It's how comfortable you feel in your own skin that really counts for anyone. It's that sense a child has of feeling in his proper place that gives him confidence and security. If a child can feel that comfort in his own skin, then he feels that he's safe; if he feels safe, then he can feel comfortable that he's competent; if he feels competent, then he can handle the world around him. But if a child's sense of **self** is disrupted by poor parental ideology, disruptive society, or unhealthy environment, nothing feels safe. Therefore, the body starts to deteriorate and the body fights back to cope or compensate for it. How many times have you heard a parent say, "Boy! Have you lost your mind?" Not only does a child sometimes not know who he is and loses his mind in some of the things he does, but a child also has no one to depend on to make the right decisions and take the right actions in the future because the people, the school system, the environment or society he is supposed to depend on for help may have put him in that mental state in the first place. As a child becomes older, we will witness the internal reactions to things that never used to faze him before; he now explodes inside when he drops a pencil. He gets tied up in knots when we can't understand what someone is saying to him in school. He gets bent out of shape over little things that we rationally know should not be bothering him. Teens will weep bitter tears for hours, if not days, over things that other people take in stride. All of these experiences tell us that the child is living in a stranger's life, and the person he was meant to be, the child he was initially born as, has abandoned himself to a society that has already lost the battle but is ruling the world.

The child is not the problem, as strongly suggested in my first book, *It's Not the Kids; It's the Parents.* Recurring patterns of problematic behaviors usually indicate that a child has an unfavorable interpretation of himself or the world in general. How a child views himself and how he views the world around him are two of the most important factors in his developmental years. A child who sees himself as persecuted will probably experience the classroom as oppressive. A child who views himself as a competitor will probably experience the world as challenging. So here are three takeaway points we can share with children to help them block the regression and maybe even rebuild a healthy self-image.

1) Stop letting people who do so little for you control your life and emotions.

Children sometimes have inordinate attachment to people who are not feeding them, clothing them, keeping a roof over their heads, paying for their cell phones, paying for their health insurance or going to help them with post high school goals or college. Sometimes these people can say things that are not true or meaningful, but painful. But let's say it is true that you have pimples on your face or you have a larger than average nose. What does that have to do with your self-worth and present or future life? Actually, in recent years, I actually adopted a new attitude toward offensive people. When someone yells at me or tries to insult me, instead of getting angry, I actually feel sorry for that person. I wonder what is presently going on or has in the past gone on for him to respond to me that way. So, don't let offensive people control your life.

2) Never sacrifice who you are just because somebody has a problem with it. Be you, always.

Just who do you think you are? And that's exactly where it should end: who *you* think you are and not what other people think you are. Now keep in mind this can be a fine line because who you are may not necessarily be who you should be, and it may need to be sacrificed for either growth or even healing. But a lot of times a child knows the difference between right and wrong, moral and immoral, ethical and unethical. but he sacrifices himself very easily, mainly because of the desire to be accepted.

Remember: The most important kind of freedom is being who you really are. When you trade in your reality for a role, the real *"you"* is never developed. We get caught up in the roles that we think we must play as dictated by society. Now granted, some roles are necessary for a short period of time. But when your role becomes your reality, that's where the problem lies.

3) We have to lose the "intention" and just do it.

Some people spend years, even decades, on intent. We fool ourselves and become satisfied with the intent. As long as we "intend" to do something, our brain takes it in as reality. Our brains can't argue the information that we give it. Therefore, anything that we tell it, it takes it in as fact. This is why action is so important. Intent is false action to the brain but acceptable. By being satisfied with intent, you give up your ability to feel, and, in exchange, you put on a mask. So, as the Nike slogan goes, "Just do it!"

"There can't be any large-scale revolution until there's a personal revolution, on an individual level. It's got to happen inside first."

Jim Morrison

"Before you diagnose yourself with depression or low self-esteem, first make sure that you are not, in fact, just surrounded by losers."

William Gibson

A popular speaker once said, "When you have to compromise who you are and your morals for the people around you, it's time to change the people around you." Part of protecting **"self"** is sometimes making that tough decision about the company you keep. Now if it is someone you just met, it is not that hard to walk away. But what if is a childhood friend? What about a family member? Human beings seem to have this desire to be accepted by as many people as possible on earth. This desire is driven by every human need to feel secure.

From the time of birth, this need is provided by mainly the maternal drive but could also be by a paternal figure. Since this need is not fulfilled by parents having to return to work in most cases, the need for security is constantly being sought for satisfaction.

Now the opposite of the seeking this security is also seen in how we handle rejection. Being rejected can destroy one's sense of security. No one wants to be called names or scorned or even disagreed with by another person. How many times has someone made a comment about another person or an event and your response was, "I know. Right?" But you really didn't feel the same way. The constant desire for security or the avoidance of rejection is not being true to self.

By not being your true "self", you are cheating the world of your contribution. In the history of the universe, there was never another you, and when you're gone, there will never be another you. What a shame that the true "you", the true "self" will never be shared! The world will never get to experience your full contribution. Everyone has his/her own interpretation of the world. Which means everyone has his own contribution. Just think how powerful we would be as a nation, as a world if everyone maximized their true self. I just recently read that Nasa's Kepler telescope just discovered over 1,200 new planets in our universe. I can't help to wonder how much sooner those planets would have been not only discovered but maybe even explored. Inhabited! If everyone had maximized his true potential. If humans had always had the ability to tap into their full self, collaborate with everyone else in the world who've done the same and truly celebrate and enjoy everything on this world and others.

In September of 1994, the hit television show *ER* aired on NBC. By the third season it was easily one of the top shows on TV. One evening, some friends of mine and I were sitting around talking about the latest episode. A few were trying not to listen because they had recorded it and not watched it yet. I think we sat around talking about the episode longer than the episode aired itself. After an hour, I noticed that my one of my friends, Stan, was off to the side not joining the conversation. Then someone had asked him, "Stan what did you think about the episode?"

With an impassive, emotionless face he returned, "I don't watch *ER*."

"What?!!" I think I heard that needle scratch the record on a cybernetic record player in the background and everything and everyone in the room got quiet...Then I thought Stan would have to run for his life as a murmur in the crowd started. "He doesn't watch *ER*...He doesn't watch *ER*...He doesn't watch *ER*..." As he kept trying to explain himself, he made this statement that was actually the beginning of a change in my mindset and life. **"Why would I spend all my time watching someone else's creativity when I have my own creativity to develop?"** That concept just totally blew my mind. I couldn't argue with that. And apparently no one else could either. Just when I thought

Stan was going to be chased out of the house with pitch forks and burning torches, the mob lulled and went back to their comfort zone. But since that night walloped me into a reality check about life and self, I have constantly been growing and challenging myself to be who I was truly meant to be. We all have to stop using the score card of others' opinions to define who we are designed from birth to be. You mean someone who doesn't pay your rent or car note, and who doesn't pay for clothes, food on the table, vacations, and kids' needs has control over your dreams and life accomplishments? Someone else's thoughts and values, likely inferior to yours, are going to determine the values you pass on to the next generation?

Though we were born with an identity separate from others, that identity quickly subconsciously fades away each and every day that we as adults don't encourage activities and experiences for children to maintain their individual identity. The basic needs of a child are more than food, clothing, and shelter. The basic needs are more than insurance, an occasional sport, dance registrations and trumpet lessons. The basic need of a child is protection. Not protection from crossing the street. Not protection from falling down stairs. Not protection from strangers. But protection from generations of preconceived ideas from families, about money, acceptance, tolerance, politics, courage, science, health, ingenuity, giving, love, and fear. You noticed in this short list I mentioned protection from "the family" and not corporate America, neighbors and friends. Everything starts from home, a future four-letter word chapter. If you take care of home, the rest of the world can't touch you.

What about different viewpoints? I love them. But opinions only truly work when there's a strong foundation of self. We don't want to be influenced by other view-points, we want to be strengthened. We want to be encouraged. We want inspiration to develop what we already have in place internally. Too many times people will listen to another source and totally change how they live. When one makes such a drastic change, it means he didn't have any true identity to start. This world has too much to offer to depend solely on us. Though you may be a Democrat you can still learn something from Republicans. Though you may be a Muslim, you can still learn something from Christianity. Though you may be from the North you can still learn from Southerners. I'm a cheese connoisseur, and I thought I knew all that there was about cheese. Just recently while watching a food channel and while working out in the gym, I saw a popular cheese in Nicaragua that had live maggots crawling all through the cheese. It was called Casu Marzu. So now I've finally heard of a cheese that I will never eat. But it was still interesting to know that cheese like that exists. This comes from different cultures and viewpoints about food.

Other viewpoints can also confirm what you're doing is the right thing and you're on track for your end goal. I'm not necessarily saying that other viewpoints are wrong; but if they are not supporting the direction that you want to go in the future, then other views can support your path.

Here are some key points in closing out this chapter. We have to be aware of how blessed you are to be here and how fragile our lives can be. When we watch the news and we see people who are dying in car accidents, natural disasters or senseless murders, why do we think it is always "the other person"? At some point in their lives don't you think that they watched the news and saw some tragedy and thought how horrible it was for "that other person"? Someone is always that "the other person." You can't even begin to take care of self if you don't respect how precious you are and start making choices that reflect that you are aware of it.

These are choices that have to do with what you are putting into your mind, ears and mouth. Also, most live a delusion, thinking that if you change the outside with certain clique of friends, clothes, hairstyles tattoos and piercings that the inner self will improve. I'm not saying that these choices are always bad. I like nice clothes as much as the next person. However, some people will spend money on tight, ill-fitting clothes instead of a gym membership or a $15 workout DVD. We must teach children to stop depending on the quick fix for approval and raising self-esteem. Stop taking care of yourself only on the outside, neglecting what is needed to go on the inside of your body.

Finally, a quote that I like is by Catherine Pulsifer: "One of the best lessons you can learn in life is to master how to remain calm." Stress and getting worked up, especially over things we have no control over, is not good for taking care of self. Stress is a big strain on almost all of your vital organs, especially the brain. If something or someone is not part of your future, then no need to stress over it or the person. As I always say, in the whole history of the universe, there never was another you and there will never be another you. You are unique and special far beyond measure. And because of your uniqueness, all that you have to offer has only one shot to introduce everything you got to the world. If you don't introduce it, it will never be known. Please, take care of your **"SELF"**. It's the only place that you truly have to live.

"WRAP"-UP

"The Teachers are afraid of the Principal; the Principal is afraid of the Superintendent; the Superintendent is afraid of the Teacher's Union; the Teacher's Union is afraid of the School Board; the School Board is afraid of the parents; the parents are afraid of the kids...the kids are afraid of no one!"

Minister Elmer Sembly, Jr.

The power of #&@%!

Let's start with profanity in itself...Why do people use profane "4 – letter words" in the first place? As far as your brain is concerned, swear words aren't even words; they are concentrated lumps of emotion. They are even stored in a completely different part of the brain from every other word we know! Formal language is stored in the Broca and Wernicke area in the brain. Swear words, however, are stored in the limbic system that controls emotions and drives. The reason why I bring this up is that we have to teach or reprogram kids' thinking. Just as profane four-letter words have an instant recall with an emotional trigger, so would a new set of four-letter words to propel a future choice and control for kids.

Most of the time, traditional four-letter words are an emotion reaction. When one is frustrated, surprised or angry, those words offer an emotional release. As any stand-up comedian can tell you, traditional four-letter words are powerful tools. More often than not, a well-placed four-letter word is the ingredient that turns a joke into comedy gold. So, using the ideas in this book, we too have to make sure that positive four-letter words are a new trigger for children. Though certain values in human life are common and core such as love, comfort and satisfaction, everyone still has his own uniqueness and individuality. This is a big commonly ignored issue in our society. People, including kids, are quickly grouped or categorized in life for either convenience or marketing purposes; and we, as adults, just follow along with it for our own convenience. Usually this is done unknowingly, and no harm is intended. When it comes to treating everyone equally or when it comes to social development, , their differences are ignored. So how do we get past the traditional view of four-letter words? How do we implement a new mindset for new four-letter words? I've created a formula to apply. It is:

$$\text{New Mindset} = \frac{\text{Work (Environment)(Love)}}{\text{Time}}$$

New mindset is equal to work, times your environment, times love for what you desire, divided by the amount of time you choose to put into it.

Everything starts with a new environment. Either mentally or physically one may have to change his surroundings. Changing your environment will also help to change your thoughts. Multiply this by the love for what you desire to accomplish in life. Take time to decide what you truly want in life. (Refer to the "Want" chapter in this book.) Divide this by the amount of time you are willing to put in. This could be anywhere from a daily life change to five minutes a day, depending on your desired end goal. Then you take the result of the combination of the environment, love and time and multiply it by WORK! Whatever result you want in life, it's going to take a great deal of work. You have to work at what you want. No matter how much hope or faith you may have, true results only come from true work. One must work to have clarity, and clarity comes from engagement and not just from idle thought and workless thought.

Our brains often confuse our memory with reality. Humans often hold on to past thoughts so firmly that daily present decisions, physical ailments and emotional stresses are based on the memory of past events. The past, which also happens to be a four- letter word, is just a term for things that no longer happen and no longer exist. Teaching this to children is easier when they are younger. However, the longer you go in sustaining improper wiring to responses of the brain, the harder it is for a child to maintain the habit of proper mental health and positive thoughts.

Yesterday ended last night! It's time to start new choices. Your choices or new choices with children should contain balance, variety, moderation. Too many people want changes overnight. The decision to make new choices can happen right now. Instantaneously. But true ever-lasting results will take some time. So many children today suffer from depression, anxieties, academic and social stresses and addictions. When a child is free of depression, anxiety, excessive stress and worry, addictions, and other psychological problems, he is more able to live his life to the fullest.

Inconvenient truths must be confronted and acted on as soon as possible. If you don't get anything else from this book, make sure that you get this next statement. **Procrastination and denial are the number one killers of achievement.** You must start doing or stop doing whatever it takes to overcome procrastination and denial. For kids, set up a reward system. Also, kids need a permanent deluge of new influences. Put them in the face of others who want to go in the same direction as your child and your family. Put them in the face of others who have already accomplished what your child has a passion for. Now is the time to take a stand on new standards.

"Don't worry about a thing.
Because every little thing, is going to be all right."

Bob Marley

Feelings are the language of the soul. Get out of your own way...and if you're a parent, get out of your kid's way. I know we all want better lives for our kids. But enabling them and constantly doing...doing...doing for them is not the answer. Let your child make mistakes...it is okay for them to feel a little pain. Nothing that is good in the history of our world has been achieved without pain. Childbirth. Salvation. Freedom of your country if you live in the US. Sport Championships. As I've said several times in both books now, IT'S EITHER THE PAIN OF DISCIPLINE OR THE PAIN OF REGRET. There is no option. It won't be easy but it is easily done. You may not know what tomorrow may bring. But you should know what you should bring. Take control. Do not let others influence you. Do not chase after anyone. Do not lead your life in the direction that you know that is not contributory to society. You can adopt this motto about negative things around you. "I don't have to let what I see be a part of me."

"This is your last chance. After this, there is no turning back. You take the blue pill, the story ends, you wake up in your bed and believe whatever you want to believe. You take the red pill, you stay in Wonderland and I show you how deep the rabbit hole goes."

Morpheus, *The Matrix 1999*

When I was a kid, for my dad and my grandparents, child psychology was found on the tree limb in the backyard. (Old School knows exactly what I'm talking about.) As I become older, though, I appreciated the love that went with it, I realized that, "Go get the switch off of the big tree out back." was not totally necessary to have a child make the right choices. Human beings have too much to offer. Don't have kids accept mediocrity. All kids, tots to teens, need guidance and support. Just because they are old enough to stay home doesn't mean they are old enough to be unsupervised. Just because they are old enough to talk doesn't mean they have to own a cell phone. Parents and children must face, decide, and then live against the pressures of a society that cares nothing about your well -being. An estimated 99% of all people and agencies use all their resources to operate and exist to keep existing...to make money for themselves...or to sustain power. As Shakespeare said in "The Merchant of Venice, "All that glitters isn't gold." Don't fall for society's enticement. Don't be lured in. Don't settle.

It is said that the last human freedom is to choose one's attitude. Take on a new one. It's time to protect your tomorrow by changing your today. As one of my mentors, Darren Hardy, said, "No matter your past, your future is spotless." When we conquer things in life, it's not the things that we are conquering. It's another part of ourselves that we are conquering. For when we conquer ourselves, that is the biggest victory of all. When we conquer things in life, we are not conquering things; we are just conquering another part of ourselves. Little by little, trial by trial, we are mastering one lost part of ourselves at a time.

The flowers of tomorrow are in the seeds of today. Everything that reproduces and grows comes from things that are existing today. And just like every flower, you will be surrounded by a lot of fertilizer. You will be rained on from time-to-time. But all of it is necessary in order to grow. But in order for it to reproduce good health, the host has to be healthy. Keep your children healthy by keeping yourself healthy. Most of a child's success in life will come from mastering the things that you don't do. We all know either deep down or even on the surface what needs to be done. And success for children isn't always mastering the great detailed and expensive things in life, it's doing the everyday simple things, mastering the little cares in life. Success in life is not what you acquire; it's what you become. Becoming more is directly proportional to achieving more. When you become more, good things will come to you whether you ask for them to or not. In my business seminars, I always say that you have to become more valuable to the market place in order to make more money. Take a company like Walmart. Isn't it safe to say that there are executives that make millions of dollars a year? Yes. Isn't it safe to say that there are employees making minimum wage? Yes. Is one person better than the other? Most definitely not? Is it possible that the executive put him/herself through additional pain and discipline to do what was necessary to get that executive job and higher pay? Most definitely.

Even when it comes to material things, I had to change my mindset on the price of things. Do they cost too much? Or is it that you just don't make enough money?...Let me help you...It's the latter. Now I did watch this show about the "wealthy" one time and in this particular restaurant there was a dessert with a price tag of $700...It had truffles and real gold in it...Now that is too much. But you get the idea.

So what new four-letter-words have you adopted? So what path are you going to take? So, more importantly, is the path you've chosen already in progress? If you were waiting for someone to come and help you get started, well I just did! There will never be that perfect time. So, you must create it! You'll never be in the mood. You'll never be smart enough, rich enough, pretty enough. Just get started. NOW.

Do you realize that billions of people every day are going to jobs that are literally making them sick? They are making choices that are making them sick. They are in relationships that are making them sick. Why would you do that to yourself? This is no secret. We see or maybe even live with people who do this to themselves, yet we teach our children to take the same path. If it hasn't worked for billions of people, why would these choices work now? Take accountability for your life. Tell your children to take responsibility for their lives and learn to be independent. Do not wait on others. Teach children to expect things to get better. Stop falling for the easy false truths in society. You're cheating the world...you're cheating yourself out of greatness by being average. Any excuse you have only sounds good and convincing to you. Any excuse your child gives only sounds good to him. No longer accept the excuses. Enough is enough.

We can only be overwhelmed by the story we attach to events and not the events themselves. We are always ready to fight the critics in front of us when it's the critic from within that's stabbing us in the back. This is why the quote in the beginning of this book by Joe DiMaggio is so important. "There are people that you are meeting or even just passing by for possibly only one time in your life..."Are you happy with what they see? Are you truly okay with what you are presently presenting to the world intentionally and unintentionally? In gratitude for your existence, you owe this world and everyone you meet your very best.

Finally, here are the **ABC Four-Letter Words of Encouragement** to get you through until volumes two and three in this series are published. Thank you for your support. I love you all, and I congratulate you now on all of your success.

You are **ABLE.** Don't let anyone tell you any other thing. It's not about being the **BEST** at any particular thing, but being the best you that you can be. As I challenge you to go through your daily new tasks, stay **CALM**; don't let the news, social media, your friends, co-workers/classmates or even family steer you away from your new life choices and **DUTY**. Always keep in mind that everything that you need to do is **EASY.** But be careful. Otherwise, you'll find out that it's even easier not to do them. Daily be honest and **FAIR** to everyone, though daily you may see that some people don't want to be fair to you. Always remember that each and every day is a **GIFT.** Maybe that's why they call it the present. Parents, remember that you are your child's first **HERO.** Please act accordingly. And just like a hero, you're never off the clock. From this day forth, daily introduce a new **IDEA** to your child. Swallow your pride because most of the good ideas may not come from you. Teach kids that life is not something you play with. It's not a **JOKE,** but you can have fun every day. As painful as it may be oftentimes, be **KIND** to everyone. The trick here is that it just has to last until you are out of their presence. **LOVE** is always the universal glue to everything. By keeping true to all these things, you'll have **MORE** abundance of all that truly matters in this world. Now don't be **NICE,** which is different from kind. People who are nice get walked on. People who are kind get results. Always stay **OPEN** - minded about all things in the beginning. Don't rush to judgment. Create careers or business where it does not feel like work, and it feels like **PLAY** along the way. Don't **QUIT** doing good to help others. You want every day to end with **REST** that you've done all that you could. But each morning you want to wake up with an impassioned **SOUL,** realizing that more for mankind needs to be done. But all and all, you want to stay **TRUE** to who you are because at the end of your life, who you were and how you made people feel is all that will really matter. There will be **UGLY,** uncontrollable events that will occur, but **VERY** much

God will reward you for staying vigilant and committed to His ultimate plan and the plan of the universe. Stay committed to knowledge and be married to wisdom. Since love is the glue to all, being **WISE** seals the edges to everything. **XOXO** to your efforts through the rest of this **YEAR** and many more to come. Be well. Be safe. Never, ever lose your faith in and **ZEST** for life.

**And as always...Peace, Love, Tranquility...
and Don't Bite Anybody!!!**

"I will not die an unlived life. I will not live in fear of falling or catching fire. I choose to inhabit my days, to allow my living to open me, to make me less afraid, more accessible; to loosen my heart until it becomes a wing, a torch, a promise. I choose to risk my significance, to live so that which came to me as seed goes to the next as blossom, and that which came to me as blossom, goes on as fruit."

Dawna Markova

**"...Only listen to yourself.
There is where you'll find the real truth."**

George Lucas

www.ingramcontent.com/pod-product-compliance
Lightning Source LLC
Chambersburg PA
CBHW072024040426
42447CB00009B/1728